WEEKEND**escape**

PRAGUE

A great weekend
in Prague

As the new wind from the West blew in, Prague underwent some quite dramatic changes. However, despite the influences of Western capitalism, it remains one of the jewels in the crown of what was once Eastern Europe, exerting a kind of fascination as an erstwhile forbidden city, now released from an oppressive regime. But Prague had a considerable life and history before the political events of the 20th century, and there is much to learn about this legendary city.

For a long time, the many buildings that are the pride of the city were covered in scaffolding or boarded up. Today, most of the restoration work is finished and the fresh-looking colorful buildings give the capital back its former splendor.

On Staroměstské náměstí (Old Town Square) you'll find an array of yellow, ocher, pink and gray buildings, all in perfect harmony. In many parts of the city, as building work is carried out and facades are repainted, gradually the old gray leaden shadows of Prague are being chased away, and a softer, pastel city is emerging.

Despite the devastating floods of August 2002, you won't see much evidence of the damage the city suffered, and it is rare now to see closed doors or barred passageways as was the case until just a few years ago. Galleries, restaurants and bars have opened their doors and the stores look inviting with brightly lit windows and tempting goods to buy. Some may say that the city is in danger of losing some of its mystery as a result, but much of Prague's past and the shadows of its musicians, writers and poets still seem to haunt the streets. The city has really changed very little and walking around, you feel as if you have just stepped onto the set of a period drama. Dip into a collection of stories

about Prague and you'll find that tales of ghosts and monsters abound, and according to folklore the buildings and the river come alive at night. Take a stroll in the castle courtyard at dusk, or walk down to the Malá Strana (Little Quarter) and across Charles Bridge (Karlův most), lined with a silent guard of honor of 30 statues along its ramparts. Continue your walk into the Staré Město (Old Town), where the bright colors of the buildings fade in the pale light of the street lamps, and narrow alleyways and passages cast their spells once more. It's a world where

time has stood still. Climb the tower of the Powder Gate, one of the few remaining parts of the Old Town's fortifications, for a fabulous view over the rooftops, before making your way to a *hospoda* or tavern to sample one of the many beers for which Prague is renowned. If you're a night owl, head for a jazz club or a nightclub. This is a great place for music lovers and there are many opportunities to listen to live performances, with regular concerts and operas held all over the city. Mozart dedicated one of his symphonies to Prague and there is a museum in his honor in the Villa Bertramka where he stayed several times on his visits here. Prague is one of Europe's smallest and most magical capitals but, despite the new Western influences, you'll find that the city's rhythm is very different from the fever pitch at which most European cities run. It developed as four separate towns and a Jewish ghetto – Hradčany, Malá Strana (Little Quarter), Staré Město (Old Town), Nové Město (New Town) and Josefov (Jewish quarter). Their medieval street plans remain largely intact, and it's here that you'll find most of the city's historical buildings and sites.

The heart of the city is the Staré Město (Old Town) with its stunning square and astronomical clock on the Old Town Hall, always a favorite with visitors. You can spend many happy hours around here, wandering through the quieter backstreets and narrow alleyways. If you want to explore farther afield, the transportation system is easy to master and excellent value. You can escape the crowds on Petřín Hill or in Vyšehrad, with views across the river toward Prague Castle which has been part of the city's skyline for over 1,000 years. Prague has a great deal to offer the visitor. Small and compact, it is full of history and mystery, so relax, soak up the atmosphere and enjoy your time in Prague.

How to get there

Climate

A flood of tourists descends on Prague from June to the end of August. Temperatures are pleasant and warm enough for the cafés to open up their terraces, but beware the sudden, sometimes violent, downpours. In the winter months, from October to March, the weather is cold and dry, sometimes sunny but mostly overcast. Temperatures can fall as low as -20°C (-4°F). If you're lucky enough to be in Prague after a snowfall, you'll see it take on a new and different kind of magic. You may even find you have the Charles Bridge to yourself. In the winter it gets dark at around 4pm, making days rather short. Spring and fall are pleasant times of year to visit and there are fewer tourists.

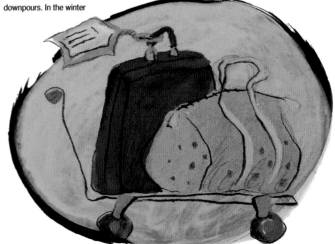

Getting there

For a great weekend in Prague, flying is the best option. Many airlines offer direct flights and you can call direct, make a reservation online or ask your travel agent.

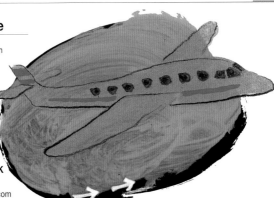

Flights from the UK
British Airways
www.british-airways.com
☎ 0870 8509850
Offers daily flights to Prague.

Easyjet
www.easyjet.com
☎ 0870 60 000 00
Daily flights from London Stansted.

ČSA (Czechoslovak Airlines)
www.csa.cz ☎ 220 104 111
There are regular flights to Prague from London Heathrow and Stansted.

From Ireland
British Airways
www.british-airways.com
☎ 0870 8509850
Offers flights from Shannon, Cork and Dublin via London Heathrow.

From the USA and Canada
ČSA (Czechoslovak Airlines)
www.csa.cz
☎ 212 765 6022
Offers a code share agreement with Delta, Crossair/Swiss and Continental. There are flights from a number of US airports via major European cities, and some airlines offer direct flights to the Czech Republic. Check the website or call for details.

British Airways
www.british-airways.com
☎ 0471 85 53 89 14
Regular flights via London from all over the USA and Canada.

Delta
www.delta.com
☎ 1 800 241 4141
Regular flights via Zurich.

From Australia and New Zealand
ČSA (Czechoslovak Airlines) offers a code share agreement with Qantas, but most of the major South Pacific airlines offer flights to Prague. From Australia you can fly with British Airways via London. From New Zealand you may have to change carrier en route. Check with your travel agent for flight details or try looking on the Internet (see box below).

By train
You can get the train to Prague from any major city in Europe. If you are traveling

SHORT BREAKS
Travel agencies often offer short-break package trips to Prague which are good value for money, with flight and accommodations in one package. Ask at your local travel agency or check on the Internet – try: www.talkingcities.co.uk or www.enroute.co.uk. Both offer all-inclusive weekend breaks.

Cheap flights
Try looking on the Internet for cheap flights – the following websites often have good deals:
www.opodo.co.uk
www.expedia.com
www.deckchair.com
www.ebookers.com
Easyjet probably offers the cheapest deals from the UK (from as little as £23 round trip), but prices rise as the flights fill up, so make your reservations well in advance.
Students under 26 looking for cheaper fares should contact their local branch of STA travel (www.sta-travel.com) or Council Travel (www.counciltravel.com).

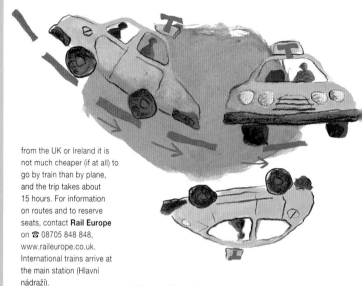

from the UK or Ireland it is not much cheaper (if at all) to go by train than by plane, and the trip takes about 15 hours. For information on routes and to reserve seats, contact **Rail Europe** on ☎ 08705 848 848, www.raileurope.co.uk. International trains arrive at the main station (Hlavní nádraží).

By bus from the UK

This is a reasonably cheap way to get to Prague from the UK (less than £100), and does not take any longer than the train. However, even with modern, well-equipped long-distance buses, the trip can be somewhat arduous. Eurolines (☎ 08705 143219) runs a regular service to Prague. Visit their website at: www.eurolines.co.uk for more information or ask at any major travel agency.

From the airport to the city center

By bus

Prague's Ruzyně airport (☎ 220 113 314, 24-hour departure and arrival information) is the only airport (*letiště*) in Prague. It is situated 20km (12 miles) west of the city. There is no metro station at the airport, so the easiest way to get to the city center is by bus 119, which terminates at Dejvická metro station (green line A). The trip takes approximately 30 minutes. Once here, take the underground and get off at Můstek station (by Wenceslas Square). You will need a Kč20 ticket for your journey, which needs to be stamped on the bus. They can be bought from the ticket office at the airport just outside the arrival hall.

By minibus

The ČEDAZ company runs a bus service carrying a maximum of six passengers and will take you to Dejvická

(line A) or to the center, stopping at Náměsti Republiky (yellow line B). The minibus leaves every 30 minutes or when it is full. The trip takes 20 minutes and you can buy your ticket on the bus (Kč90).

By taxi

The taxi company Airport Cars owns the monopoly on taxi runs from the airport and operates a pass system which varies according to the days

and times. Taxis wait outside the arrival hall and will charge you around Kč600 to Kč700 to get to the city center. To come back, contact a cheaper taxi firm like AAA (☎ 14 014).

Formalities

EU citizens can travel to Prague without restriction. Only a valid identity card or passport is needed. Americans and Canadians can travel to Prague without a visa as long as they are planning to stay less than 180 days; after this 180-day period a visa is necessary. You must

also insure that your passport is valid before you go. Citizens of New Zealand can travel to Prague without a visa if they intend to stay less than 90 days. Australian citizens require a tourist visa valid for up to 30 days, which should be obtained from your embassy at home before departing (see p. 9 for addresses). You can also obtain a multiple-entry 90-day visa.

Customs

When you enter the Czech Republic, personal goods are not subject to customs duty. The duty-free allowance is 90 liters of wine, 10 liters of spirits and 800 cigarettes. Customs require an export licence for expensive goods such as antiques. For more information on antiques, contact the Museum of Decorative Arts (Uměleckoprůmyslové): Ul. 17 Lipostadu 2, ☎ 251 093 111. For paintings and statues, contact the National Gallery (Sternberg Palace) at: Hradčanské 15, ☎ 233 250 068. For information on exporting coins, contact Národní Museum (National Museum): Václavské náměstí 68, ☎ 224 497 111.

NATIONAL HOLIDAYS

New Year's Day (Jan. 1);
Easter Monday;
Labor Day (May 1);
VE Day (May 8);
Remembrance of the Slavonic Missionaries (July 5);
Anniversary of the death of Jan Hus in 1415 (July 6);
National Day (Sep. 28);
Foundation of the Republic in 1918 (Oct. 28);
Commemoration of the Struggle for Freedom and Democracy (Nov. 17);
Christmas Eve, Christmas Day and Boxing Day (Dec. 24-26)

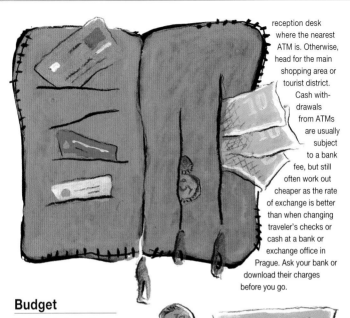

reception desk where the nearest ATM is. Otherwise, head for the main shopping area or tourist district. Cash withdrawals from ATMs are usually subject to a bank fee, but still often work out cheaper as the rate of exchange is better than when changing traveler's checks or cash at a bank or exchange office in Prague. Ask your bank or download their charges before you go.

Budget

You'll have to allow quite a large budget for your accommodations. Hotels are very expensive in Prague, just as they are in any other European capital. Allow Kč3,000 per night for a double room with bath in the historic center (Prague 1).

On the other hand, eating local dishes in the *hospodas* will cost you around Kč150. You'll be able to go to a theater, nightclub or concert without going bankrupt as ticket prices and drinks are generally reasonably priced.

Local currency

The local currency is the Czech *koruna* (Kč). Notes come in denominations of Kč50, Kč100, Kč200, Kč500, Kč1,000, Kč2,000 and Kč5,000 and coins Kč1, Kč2, Kč5, Kč10, Kč20 and Kč50. There's no restriction on

bringing Czech currency in and out of the country but it's probably best to buy your crowns once you get there and use them up before returning home.

Exchanging money

Payment by credit card is not as widespread in the Czech Republic as it is in the US or the UK. Therefore, it is advisable to carry cash with you to pay for the restaurant check, for example, or for small souvenirs. You won't have any problems withdrawing money, whatever card you may be using: Ask a local or someone at your hotel

Packing your suitcase

If you're visiting Prague in the summer, just pack normal light clothing. Don't forget to pack a pair of comfortable walking shoes. This is a city to explore on foot, and the cobbled streets can be very uneven. If you are visiting in winter, take a hat, a scarf, a warm coat and waterproof shoes. It can get very cold! The cafés, restaurants and hotel rooms are often overheated, so wear layers of clothes you can peel off easily. Whatever the season, remember to pack a smart outfit for a visit to the opera or to a concert. When it snows in the winter, carry your evening

ISIC CARD

Students and others under 26 should obtain an ISIC Card (International Student Identity Card) which gets you discounts on transportation, museum entry and shows. You should be able to obtain one from specialist student travel agencies, such as STA or Council Travel.

shoes in a bag and put them on in the cloakroom on arrival – this is what the locals do.

Health and insurance

If you pay for your ticket by credit card, you automatically benefit from some insurance regarding your luggage, the possible cancellation of your trip and medical repatriation. Find out more from your credit card company or ask your bank. EU citizens can also reclaim medical expenses once back in the UK; make sure you take a European Health Insurance Card with you (forms available from post offices). Non-EU citizens should make sure they have adequate cover. The cost is low but it offers real benefits in case of problems.

Take a supply of your own prescription medicines, as you may not be able to find exactly the same in Prague. For general requirements, there are 24-hour pharmacies at Palackého 5, ☎ 224 946 981, and at Belgická 37, ☎ 222 519 731.

Local time

Prague is on Central European Time (GMT plus one hour)

except from the end of March to the end of September, when Summer Time takes effect (GMT plus two hours). This is six hours ahead of New York and nine hours ahead of Los Angeles.

Language

Czech is the national language, but you'll find that English and German are often understood, which is helpful as Czech is not the easiest language to understand or speak!

Personal safety

Crime has risen in Prague since the fall of Communism, but mostly involves theft rather than physical aggression. It is worth taking

the following precautions:
• Leave valuables and important papers in the hotel safe. Carry a photocopy of your passport with you.
• When parking the car, don't leave anything visible.
• If you do have something stolen, report it to the police.
• Be aware of pickpockets, especially in tourist areas. Keep your wallet or purse behind a zipped internal compartment of your bag or coat if possible.

Voltage

The electrical supply is 220 volts, as in the rest of Europe, and Czech plugs have two round pins. Bring an adaptor with you for British and North American plugs.

USEFUL ADDRESSES

Czech embassies
UK and Ireland
26 Kensington Palace Gardens, London W8 4QY
☎ 020 7243 1115
www.czechembassy.org.uk
USA
3900 Spring of Freedom St NW, Washington DC 20008
☎ 202 966 8540
email: washington@embassy.mzv.cz
Canada
541 Sussex Drive, Ottawa, Ontario, K1N 6Z6
☎ 613 562 3875
Australia
8 Culgoa Circuit, O'Malley, Canberra, ACT 2606
☎ 02 6290 1386
New Zealand
48 Hair Street, PO Box 43035, Wainuiomata, Wellington
☎ 04 564 6001

Official tourism websites:
www.czechtourism.com
www.prague-info.cz
www.pis.cz
www.touristoffices.org.uk/Czech_Republic/index.html
For embassies and consulates in Prague, see p. 33.

Musical
tradition

You'll be surrounded by music wherever you go in Prague – it's an integral part of the Czech character. You'll hear it in churches, most of which are now concert halls, in gardens during the summer months, on Charles Bridge and in the Old Town Square. You'll never be far from a performance of a sonata or requiem, and you'll soon appreciate the local saying that there's a musician lurking inside every Czech citizen.

Europe's conservatoire of music

The English composer Charles Burney was so impressed in 1772 by the knowledge and technical skill of the musicians he met in Prague that he called the city the "conservatoire of Europe." This turned out to be a premonition – the first conservatoire subsequently opened its doors here in 1811. The Museum of Musical

Instruments, which houses 3,000 pieces, is another testimony to just how musical the city is. Unfortunately, it is currently closed to the public. It was housed by the Order of Malta for many years, but it is now looking for new premises.

National treasures

The musician Bedřich Smetana (1824–1884) did most to put the Czech national identity on the musical map. He was the first composer to integrate popular songs and dances into his classical works, of which the most famous are *The Bartered Bride* and *My Fatherland*. This tradition was continued by Antonín Dvořák (1841–1904), the famous composer of the *New World Symphony*, Leoš Janáček (1854–1928) and Bohuslav Martinů (1890–1959).

Mozart, freeman of Prague

Prague has a strong tradition of celebrating not just its own national geniuses but also those of foreign countries, such as Beethoven, Liszt, Chopin,

Berlioz and Mozart. An Austrian tired of being misunderstood by his Viennese public, Mozart decided to give the first performance of *The Marriage of Figaro* in Prague. A warm welcome awaited him, and he was so overwhelmed by the ovation that he made his famous announcement: "My fellow citizens of Prague understand me." The much-loved Mozart came to Prague only four times, but the Mozart Museum is here, located in Bertramka (Mozartova 169, Prague 5, ☎ 257 318 461, every day 9am-6pm, 4pm Nov.-Mar.; concerts Wed. and Sat. at 7pm; www.bertramka.cz). It is in this house where his musician friends, the Dušek, used to live, that he finished writing *Don Giovanni*, which was first performed at the Estates Theater in 1787 (see p. 55).

Prague Spring Music Festival

Established in 1946, this prestigious festival opens annually on May 12, the

anniversary of the death of Bedřich Smetana. After the ritual Mass has taken place at his grave, his great symphony *My Fatherland* is played in the Municipal House (Obecní Dům), in the room named after him. Beethoven's *Ninth Symphony* closes the event on June 3.

The Czech Philharmonic Orchestra

Václav Talich, Rafael Kubelík and Karel Ancerl are among the famous conductors who have contributed to the orchestra's reputation, and Antonín Dvořák

himself conducted the first concert on January 4 1896. Unfortunately, Gerd Albrecht, the German conductor appointed in 1992, had to relinquish his post in 1995 due to "nationalist" pressures. Ironically enough, he was promptly replaced by a Russian, Vladimír Ashkenazy. There are two other official orchestras, the Prague Symphony and the radio orchestra. However, there are also dozens of other unofficial ones, including several chamber music groups. Quatuor Talich deserves a mention, being among the best of these.

BUILD UP YOUR MUSIC COLLECTION

Supraphon:
Here you can buy a set of 8 CDs with historical recordings of the Czech Philharmonic Orchestra, conducted by Václav Talich; *Káťa Kabanová* by Leoš Janáček (Czech Philharmonic Orchestra directed by Sir Charles Mackerras); *Greek Passions* by Bohuslav Martinů (National Philharmonic Orchestra of Brno, directed by Sir Charles Mackerras).

Multisonic:
Try *Vaňhal, Mysliveček and Vent*, *"Mozart and his Czech friends"* (Virtuosi di Praga Ensemble, conducted by Oldřich Vlček).

Studio Matouš:
Here we suggest *Missa sanctissimae trinitatis*, by Jan Zelenka (Musica Florea Ensemble, conducted by Marek Štryncl).

Prague,
queen of Baroque

You'll come across Baroque architecture all over Prague. There are exotic churches, grand palaces and innumerable statues. The great paradox is that Baroque architecture was something that was imposed on Prague, as a weapon in the fight against Protestantism. However, the city managed to integrate this architectural style successfully, and it eventually became an expression of the Czech national spirit.

How Baroque art came to Prague

The defeat at the Battle of the White Mountain in 1620 made Bohemia a province of Austria. Under the Catholic Hapsburg rule Prague was totally reshaped. The citizens of Prague saw the Reformation as an attack on their city which was demonstrated very graphically by the construction of the Klementinum by the Jesuits who destroyed 32 houses, two gardens, three churches and a Dominican convent to make space for it. The intellectual élite was banished, and Prague fell under a dark Baroque spell, which was to be used against the former religion.

Artistic influences

Two strong artistic influences came together in Prague. The marriage between the classical style from Austria and France and a Baroque style of Italian and German origin took place between 1700 and 1740 against the perfect backdrop of the city, with its wonderfully appropriate dramatic terrain.

Braun and Brokof

There are more statues in Prague than in any other city in the world. They're on the facades of homes and churches and in the squares, and are the city's most characteristic Baroque feature. Many of them were the inspiration of two key figures, Mathias Bernard Braun and Ferdinand Maximilien Brokof. Braun and Brokof were contemporaries, born in 1684 and 1688 respectively, and they both died of lung disease caused by their years of stone cutting. Don't miss the statue of St Luitgard on Charles Bridge, the 12th statue on the right starting from the Old Town. Sculpted by Braun in 1710, it is a voluptuous pastiche of Bernini. In the following year Brokof sculpted the statue of St Frances Xavier, fifth on the left.

Like father, like son

Kristof Dientzenhofer (1655–1722) came from a family of Bavarian masons, and, together with his son Kilian

Ignaz (1689–1751) and the latter's son-in-law, Anselmo Lurago, they gave Prague its most beautiful Baroque buildings. They were responsible for the facades of the Loreto and the Church of St Nicholas in the Old Town (not to be confused with the Church of St Nicholas in the Little Quarter, the magnificent creation of the same dynasty).

Where to find Baroque architecture

You won't have to go far to discover the Baroque in Prague. You'll see grand palaces, smaller houses and statues on churches, all Baroque in style. If you wander around the Malá Strana (Little Quarter) and Staré Město (Old Town), you will come across many Baroque buildings. Not to be missed are the following: Klementinum (see p. 52), St Nicholas's in the Malá Strana (see p. 46) and the Loretto (see p. 40), Buquoy Palace (see p. 49), Wallenstein Palace (see p. 47), Charles Bridge (see p. 50), Nerudova Street (see p. 46) and Villa Amerika (Dvořák Museum, see p. 65).

A neo-Baroque designer

Bořek Šípek takes you back to the Baroque era with his padded armchairs, straight from the time of Mozart, and his extravagant colored glass vases. He was exiled to Germany in 1968, and then to Holland in 1983, finally returning to Prague after the Velvet Revolution in 1989. Since 1992 he has been in charge of the reconstruction of Prague Castle. Šípek is an accomplished and eclectic artist, who has been responsible for the refurbishment of the Karl Lagerfeld shops all over the world. He has also created the design of the first porcelain table service to be commissioned by the Sèvres manufacturers since the 18th century.

A BAROQUE CITY

"Prague is a naturally Baroque city, where streets mingle like voices, where the traveler is constantly surprised by its sensuality and seduced by its luscious curves, at every sudden turning or hidden corner."

Petr Král

Prague in 1900:
Secession and cubism

At the turn of the 19th and 20th centuries, an overwhelming explosion of creativity launched Prague to the forefront of European art. The Czech Secession movement has its origins in Germany's Jugendstil, Austria's own Secession and France's art nouveau. There are over 300 art nouveau-style buildings in the city. Above all, don't miss the Europa Café.

Art nouveau

First displayed at the Jubilee Exhibition in 1891, art nouveau is characterized by its curved sinuous lines and its floral motifs. It was a reaction against the academic establishment.

A total art form

Art nouveau became a total art form and influenced not only architecture and painting but also decorative arts. Stained-

glass windows, wallpaper, mosaics, furniture and jewelry were all involved in what became not just an art form but a way of life.

Alphonse Mucha, art nouveau artist

Alphonse Mucha, born in 1860 in Moravia, is the most famous Czech artist and one of the most successful exponents of the art nouveau style. The natural world was the inspiration for his exotic figures with their flowing hair, often set against floral backgrounds with tentacle-like forms. It was in Paris in 1894 that Mucha became famous through a poster designed for Sarah Bernhardt. A painter, illustrator, sculptor and creator of stylized clothes and jewelry, he was turned down by the Academy and left Prague at the age of 19. He returned to live in the city in 1910, and was commissioned to decorate the Mayor's room in the Municipal House. Don't miss the Mucha Museum which opened in 1998 (see Don't Miss p. 70). The museum shop has some wonderful Mucha-inspired gifts and art books.

Art Décoratif

Melantrichova 5
☎ 224 222 283
Every day 10am-8pm.
Art Décoratif is well worth a visit. Here you will find wonderful copies of art-nouveau items, some of them made by Alphonse Mucha's own granddaughter. There's a huge selection of art-nouveau lamps and replicas of Mucha's jewelry, such as the butterfly brooch designed for Sarah Bernhardt. An art-deco set of six glasses and a decanter will cost around Kč3,600. A limited series vase will set you back Kč12,000, and for the superb replicas of the wall lamps

designed for the Municipal House you will pay as much as Kč41,000.

Baba Villas

The small Baba district is a little out of the way but well

worth the trip. There are 33 villas, built between 1928 and 1933 by members of the Czech architectural avant-garde (including Josef Gočar and Adolf Loos), and conceived as a "Constructivist colony" by Pavel Janák, born-again functionalist. Take tram 20 or 25 to the area and look out for the following streets: Na Babě, Nad Patankou, Jarní, Přehledová. Unfortunately, the houses aren't open to the public, so you'll have to content yourself with their external architecture only. Some of the houses have been altered but others remain just as they were originally.

Cubism

From 1910 onward, Prague gave in to the cubist influence, which came about as a

reaction to the soft, curved lines of the art nouveau style. Braque and Picasso were the founders of the movement. The group of "Plastic Artists," as they were then called, took on the help of the architects Josef Chochol, Josef Gočar and Pavel Janák to work on cubist buildings. These are located at the foot of the Vyšehrad (see p. 66). See works by Picasso and Czech cubist artists at the Modern Art Museum (see Don't Miss p. 68).

AN ART NOUVEAU DAY OUT

Having reached the main **station** (Wilsonova 8/300), you can enjoy breakfast at the **Europa Hotel**, gather your thoughts in front of the Jan Hus Monument, by Ladislav Šaloun, and then make your way to the **Mucha Museum**. Have a bite for lunch at the **Hotel Paříž**, and dedicate your afternoon to a visit of the **Museum of Decorative Arts** (see p. 51). In the evening go to a concert and then dinner at the **Obecní dům** (see p. 55). Finish your evening off with a nightcap at the **Lucerna Bar** (see p. 61), the perfect end to an "art nouveau" day.

Kafka, Hašek, Hrabal:
Prague's great figures

Prague has been visited by and written about by many international authors, but it has its own literary giants, among them Hašek, Hrabal and, of course, Kafka. Kafka is an extremely popular figure with tourists, and references to him are everywhere in the city. His writing was influenced greatly by Prague, of which he said that it "never lets go of you… this little mother has claws. We ought to set fire to it at both ends, on Vyšehrad and Hradčany, and maybe then it might be possible to escape."

Franz Kafka

Born in Prague in 1883 into a Jewish family, Kafka is without doubt the most famous Czech author. A member of the German-speaking Jewish community, he wrote in German, and his works *The Trial* and *Metamorphosis* are both internationally renowned. He spent the majority of his life around Josefov, the old Jewish quarter, but gradually the ghetto disappeared and a

new city emerged, in which he no longer felt at ease. "The unhealthy old Jewish ghetto within us is more real that the new hygienic one that surrounds us," said Kafka in 1902. He frequented literary salons, including the Café Louvre, the Savoy, the Café Arco and the Slavia, where he enjoyed spirited debates with intellectuals and artists. At Café Stefan the first reading of *Metamorphosis* took place, presented by Ernst Pollack.

Before Kafka died in 1924, he asked his friend Max Brod to burn all his work. Luckily, Brod disobeyed, and the majority of Kafka's work was published after his death.

Jaroslav Hašek

Hašek was Kafka's contemporary. Born in the same year, 1883, he wrote *The Good Soldier Švejk*. Writer, journalist, great orator, bigamist and People's Commissar in the Red Army, Hašek was a great humorist and one of Prague's colorful characters. He spent much of his time in taverns and bars, and was snubbed by the intellectual circles of Prague. Despite this, *The Good Soldier Švejk* became a highly popular play throughout Central Europe. Hašek died at the age of 40, and it was left to a friend to complete the last volume of the adventures of the naive but artful soldier. His work is one of the greatest achievements of Czech literature, with its humour and its echoes of *Don Quixote* and *Sancho Panza*.

were indeed published from 1963 onward, to critical and public acclaim. He became the most successful Czech author of the 1960s, with works including *Closely Watched*

Trains, which was made into an equally brilliant film by Jiří Menzel. He wrote *The Little Town Where Time Stood Still*, *Dancing Lessons, Too Loud a Solitude* and *I Served the King of England*. His works combined poetry and comedy with a touch of Prague's idiosyncratic humor and a good dash of slang. His death on February 3 1997 shocked the country, when he fell from the sixth floor of the Bulovka Hospital in Prague. If you want to know more about his world before embarking on his writings, enjoy a beer in the Golden Tiger tavern (see p. 53), where he spent much of his time.

Bohumil Hrabal

Bohumil Hrabal was born in 1914, and in 1946 he became a doctor of law, a career he did not pursue. Instead, his many career moves included railroad worker, commercial traveler, steel factory worker, packer and theater extra. He spent a good deal of his time watching, listening and writing. He had no real intention of being published and was inspired by human nature and conversations in bars. However, many of his works

IN KAFKA'S FOOTSTEPS

Make a quick pilgrimage to the Old Town Square (Staroměstské náměstí). Kafka was born in Maiselova, to the left of St Nicholas's Church. From 1893 to 1901, he studied at Kinský Palace, the former German language imperial school, at no. 12 on the square. The Kafka family lived in the house at no. 3 (Dům U Minuty), decorated with sgraffiti, and at Celetná 3, close to the Gothic church. Kafka's grave is in the new Jewish cemetery of Olšány (metro A, Želivského station).

Glass and
crystal

Bohemian glass has ranked among the finest in the world since the 14th century, rivaling its Venetian and Baccarat counterparts. It is made of a mixture of metal and Bohemian sand, and its exact composition is a secret closely guarded by the Czech master glassmakers. The only known fact is that they don't use lead.

Bohemian glass

Glass has been made in Bohemia since the early Middle Ages. It was used on bracelets and necklaces, and it was blown to make glasses. You can see it in the lovely mosaic on the south portal of St Vitus Cathedral. In the 16th century, the Hapsburg court began demanding more sophisticated pieces, and the artists responded with Renaissance-style objects, inspired by Venetian crystal. Toward 1600, Rudolph II's jeweler, Caspar

Lehmann, experimented with a technique used only in precious stone engraving, involving bronze and copper wheels. Thanks to him, the art of engraving glass took off in Bohemia. Glasses with polished stems and Baroque designs and goblets made of finely cut glass engraved with floral motifs are now exported throughout the world.

Achieving perfection

From 1720, glassworkers began to gild and paint their creations, which were soon more prized than those made in Venice. In the following century, the color, detail and pattern all improved dramatically. Empire and Biedermeier styles became

fashionable, resulting in finely shaped, engraved glass. Europe began to discover the East, and Count Georg Buquoy developed a technique of making thick, opaque glass, which he then embellished with Chinese motifs and encrusted with agate and rubies. Bohemian crystal became famous for its exquisite plates, glass jewelry and mirrors. In the 20th century, the designs came under the influence of art nouveau and cubist styles, which resulted in some very avant-garde pieces. There was a wonderful sense of creativity in the air. Even today the pieces made during this period appear very bold and continue to inspire modern designers throughout the world.

The history of lead

The customary method of making crystal includes lead. It is lead which makes the glass softer, easier to engrave and to cut. Its luminosity is increased as more lead is added. Some Czech master glassworkers continue to work without lead, as was the tradition in former times. The famous Moser glassworks is one such company. They replace the lead with a complex chemical composition, which gives the glass clarity, quality and strength. In Prague, fine examples of leadfree glass can command prices as high as their French or English equivalents.

Lead content in crystal

The long-term effects of lead on alcohol and the resulting risk to health have yet to be proven. It is advisable not to keep alcohol in a crystal decanter for too long as small particles may penetrate the liquid. According to the criteria set down by the European Union, glass contains less than four percent lead, crystal more than ten percent and very high-quality crystal at least 30 percent. Baccarat crystal from France contains 34 percent. In the Czech Republic real crystal has a lead content of at least 24 percent. Crystalline contains less lead but more barium oxide, which gives it the required color and luminosity.

MUSEUM AND SHOP

**Uměleckoprůmyslové Muzeum
(Museum of Decorative Arts)**
This museum houses collections of furniture, posters, ceramics and porcelain, but that's not all. You'll be able to learn the art of Bohemian glassmaking from the Middle Ages to the present day and see a stunning collection of art-deco pieces.
**Ul. 17. listopadu 2, Prague 1; ☎ 251 093 265
Tue.-Sun. 10am-6pm (8pm Tue., free entry 5-8pm).**

Moser
To discover Bohemian crystal, don't hesitate to visit this elegant shop with its exquisite wood panels and stained-glass decorations. Created in 1857 in Karlovy Vary, Moser became famous for the delicacy and the purity of its crystalware. Certain of the exhibits – some of which are precious antiques – are of such outstanding beauty they deserve to be in a museum.
**Na příkopě 12, Černá Ruže (inside the shopping center),
Prague 1; ☎ 224 211 293
Mon.-Fri. 10am-8pm, Sat.-Sun. 10am-7pm.**

Prague's passion
for puppets

Prague is a puppet paradise. You will find them everywhere, as popular and well-loved today as they were 200 years ago. It's not surprising to learn that the international puppet society was established in Prague in 1929, raising the status of the puppet industry to that of an art form. The organization now boasts more than 8,000 members in a total of 77 countries.

A foreign import

What has now become a national passion for puppets was originally imported into Bohemia after the Thirty Years' War (1618–1648), by English, German and Italian troops. Toward the end of the 18th century, the Czechs began to make their own puppets, reinforcing their sense of national identity.

The golden age

At the turn of the 19th and 20th centuries, the puppet theater

underwent a "renaissance" of its own. Artists and designers, such as the painters Vít Skála and Ota

Bubeníček and the sculptor Ladislav Šaloun, confirmed it as a valid art form. In 1911, the "Czech Union of Friends of the Puppet" was launched to be followed by the *Czech Puppet Magazine* in 1912. In the 1920s many hundreds of theater societies and schools were formed, and the popularity of the puppet really took off.

"Aleš Puppets"

The painter Mikuláš Aleš (1852–1913) was renowned for his frescoes, which were seen in many Prague homes. However, at the beginning of the 20th century he created his famous "Aleš Puppets." His original intention was merely to entertain his children with his naive cardboard figures and their oversized heads. His designs then became the model for the first mass-produced Czech puppets. They came onto the market in 1912 and are still a commercial success. Look closely at the "wise man with the white beard" puppet because this is a self-portrait of the artist himself.

Špejbl and Hurvínek

The best-known puppet show in the city is held at the Špejbl and Hurvínek theater (Divadlo Špejbla a Hurvínka). Špejbl is the unrepentant father of Hurvínek, his reprobate son who has a falsetto voice. They are instantly recognizable with their huge rustic clogs and were conceived in the 1920s by Josef Škupa (1892–1957). They are now stars of the small screen, having been

immortalized by Jiří Trnka, the famous maker of animated films.

Little Gaspard

In this puppet play there are 12 protagonists, made up of

Guignol, the devil, Death, six male characters and three female ones. They vary in size and are all-string marionettes. Guignol, the Mr. Punch figure, was adopted by the Czech public in 1810 and renamed "Little Gaspard" or Kašpárek.

Marionette Theater

Created in 1911, the Prague National Marionette Theater

played its part in the revival of the great Czech tradition of study and learning. The majority of the 50 members of the troupe hold diplomas in the art of puppet theater from an academy of dramatic art. If you are a purist, you won't want to miss the most famous pieces in the repertory. *Don Giovanni* was written in 1782, five years before the opening of Mozart's opera in Prague.

For information and tickets: Via Praga, Žatecka 1 and Celetná 13, Prague 1, ☎ 224 819 322 or 224 819 323.

POD LAMPOU PUPPET SHOP

In a tiny shop at the foot of the Charles Bridge, you will find wooden, ceramic and plaster puppets, all suspended from the ceiling. It opened in 1994 and is designed to look like a dollhouse. The owner, Pavel Truhlar, has enormous respect for the quality of the little figures he sells and only buys from handpicked artists. Choose from over 1,500 models, in the price range Kč190–17,000.

U Lužického semináře 5
☎ 606 924 392; www.loutky.com
Every day 11am-8pm
Additional address: Ungelt – Týn 1.

Bohemian
garnets

Bohemia is known for its semiprecious stones, and craftsmen have been working with garnets for many years. Garnet is extracted in the north of the Czech Republic, in Turnov, not far from Český Ráj, which means "Czech paradise." It remains one of the most sought-after stones.

A short history of garnet

Until the Middle Ages, garnet was used for medicinal purposes as well as being set as jewelry. At the end of the 16th century, it became fashionable to set the stone in rings, as was the practice in Turnov from the beginning of the 17th century. Rudolph II, the Archduke of Austria, German Emperor and King of Hungary and Bohemia, was one of the first admirers of the stone, and he had a beautiful collection of uncut and worked garnets. In 1609, Boetius de Boot, the Emperor's doctor, confirmed that Rudolf indeed owned one of the largest garnet stones in the land.

International fame

The reputation of garnet spread outside the kingdom of Bohemia, and demand grew for it accordingly. In 1785, 187 jewelers were working with the stone in the Czech workshops. Seven years later, the total was 259. There is a story that the ladies of the Russian court wore Turnov garnets in 1815 at the Vienna Congress to celebrate the defeat of Napoleon. The jewels traveled around the world and were seen at major exhibitions.

There is a record of the unusual presence of Bohemian goldsmiths in Berlin in 1844, when they displayed their work there. Similarly, in Amsterdam in 1883, the Kratochvil company won the silver medal for one of its pieces.

Garnets with everything!

At the end of the 19th century, production diversified and garnets began to play a major part in the composition of the jewelry itself rather than simply as decoration. The settings became much more subtle and the metal component barely visible. The stone was so fashionable at the time that it became used in letter openers, photograph frames, paper knives, powder compacts and cigarette cases. From 1900, jewelers began to work in the art nouveau style. Floral and ornamental motifs were incorporated into the design of brooches, combs and pendants, in which the garnets were set. This fashionable jewelry was exported all over the world and helped establish the international reputation of the Bohemian garnet.

Garnets today

Take a look in the jewelry store windows in Prague, and you'll find garnets of all shapes and sizes. On sale are rings, earrings, brooches, bracelets, pendants, lucky charms, hearts and crosses. They tend to be rather classic in style but still retain a certain charm. A Czech garnet bought today could still remind you of your grandmother, since even contemporary pieces have a nostalgic feel about them. The balance between settings and stones has changed little since the end of the 19th century. The setting is often virtually hidden beneath all the small stones.

A lucky stone

Mysterious powers have long been attributed to the garnet. Deep red in color but at the same time almost transparent, it can look like a drop of blood, which is why it has been thought to have healing powers and to bring strength, energy, courage and even a happy temperament to those who wear it. As a symbol of blood, the garnet has been associated with the mystery of the Eucharist, and it often adorns liturgical pieces. The Strahov Monastery has good examples of this use, with its decorated gilded monstrances and crosses (Klášter Premonstrátů na Strahově, Strahovské nádvoří, Prague 1, open Tue.-Sun. 9am-noon and 1-5pm, entrance charge).

GARNET CRAFTSMEN

The craftsmen's cooperative, known as *Granát*, is based in Turnov, garnet capital of Bohemia. It still makes traditional Czech jewelry today, and its current collection stands at 3,500 models. However, don't expect them to be very fashionable. Most of the settings are in silver, silver-gilt or in 14/18 carat gold. You can try on pieces and purchase them from *Granát Turnov* (Dlouhá 28–30, Staré Město, see p. 105).

Beer,
elixir of truth and life

At 161 liters per capita per year, Czechs hold the world record for the consumption of beer. This isn't really surprising when you learn that the word *pivo*, which describes the national beverage, comes from the verb *pití*, meaning to drink, which is an activity that is central to Prague life. A "Friends of Beer Party" was formed during the elections in 1990 and managed to recruit many thousands of members to its cause.

The Big Two

Among the 400 brands of local beer, the most famous is the Plzeňský prazdroj ("original source"), better known by its German name Pilsner Urquell. The Bavarian brewer, Josef Groll, first made the beer in 1842 in the town of

Czechs and their beer

Beer has been consumed in Bohemia since the 11th century and reached the height of its popularity in the 13th century, thanks to King Václav I, who officially abolished the ban on brewing. It had carried the penalty of excommunication, although

this was accorded very little respect. The unique quality of the beer is said to result from the perfect harmony between the barley used for making malt, the fine Bohemian hops and the extraordinarily soft local spring water. Since the 14th century, Bohemia has justifiably been acclaimed as the source of some of the best beers in the world.

Plzen (in German, Pilsen), located 80km (50 miles) from Prague. Its exceptional qualities explain why it has become a generic term, with Pils, Pilsner or Pilsener denoting a light beer with a distinctive hop flavor resulting from a second fermenting at low temperatures. Its only rival is Budvar or Budweiser brewed in České Budějovice (in German, Budweis), south of Prague. This is no relation to the American beer of the same name, although there are frequent disputes as to which of the brewing giants owns the copyright of the trademark.

And one very special beer...

U Fleků, at Křemencova, 11, is a classic beer hall where the house beer has been brewed since 1499 and is still sold there today. It is a unique, strong and slightly sweet dark beer and large quantities are made each year and sold exclusively on these premises. Visit the beer garden in the summer and you will think you are at a tavern in Bavaria. One of the vaulted rooms has a cabaret at night.

Beer you won't find elsewhere

There are three other famous local beers that you should try on your trip – Staropramen, Braník and Pražan. Taste the local brews, Krušovice and Velkopopovický kozel. The latter is quite a strong beer and is easily recognizable by its label, showing a goat holding a glass of beer and no doubt the animal helps to add his own particular flavor to the brew!

How to drink beer in Prague

Beer should be served at cellar temperature and with a head. To check its quality, see if a match can remain upright in the froth for ten seconds. After you have ordered and finished your first beer, your glass will be replaced automatically by the waiter, who marks a tab on the table. It is up to you to put a stop to the flow and to avoid becoming "as drunk as a Dane," as the locals say.

It's all in the percentages

If you buy bottled beer, remember that the most obvious figure on the label (usually 10 percent or 12 percent) is not a reference to the alcohol content but rather to the density of malt used in the brew. The percentage of alcohol by volume is either in smaller type or not shown at all. As a general rule, divide the density by three to work out the alcohol content. Beers can be bought in cans but these are principally for export. Local connoisseurs don't drink canned beer.

BRIEF GLOSSARY OF TERMS FOR THE BEER DRINKER

Pivo: beer.
Velké pivo: large beer (50cl or just under a pint).
Malé pivo: small beer (30cl, larger than a half pint).
Pivnice: polite word for a pub or beer hall. Usual word is *hospoda* and *hostinec*. *Pivovar* is a generic term, meaning a pub.
Pivní sýr: soft and extremely pungent cheese mixed with chopped onions, paprika, then drowned in beer.
Tekutý chléb: local name for beer, meaning "liquid bread."

Shall we dance?

Jan Neruda, poet and journalist, wrote widely about Prague. He captured the importance of dance, an essential part of Prague life and not just a pastime, when he said that "the whole country sparkled like a ballroom dance floor and everyone danced on its musical soil." The dance tradition began over a century ago, and is still immensely popular today. Every dance association makes it a point of honor to organize its own ball. Learning to dance when young is still considered a vital social skill.

Those first steps...

The Austrian aristocracy first held glamorous balls at the beginning of the 18th century in Prague's many palaces. A century later there were more than 20 dance halls in the city. People danced the polonaise, the gavotte and the waltz, but soon the Czechs had mastered these and were ready to invent their own dances, such as the Česká beseda and the polka.

Dancing for your country

The waltz took on a clearly political overtone through its strong links with the intense revival of the national movement at the beginning of the 19th century. From 1840, fervent patriots took a stand with the organization of the first "Czech balls." Thanks to the success of a major event organized in April 1848, the National Theater was constructed with funds from private donations. Bedřich

Smetana was an ardent nationalist, and dance became one of his favorite themes. In the greatest Czech opera,

The Bartered Bride, Smetana took popular polka tunes and reworked them, making a tribute at the end of the first act to this very energetic dance. Smetana was a German speaker but was still the most nationalist of Czech composers.

Learning to dance

Learning to dance the revered polka and with it the waltz, tango, rumba and paso doble, not to mention rock 'n' roll, is an integral part of Prague education, and boys and girls aged 15 to 17 are signed up for *Taneční* (dance classes). The first ball offers them an opportunity to demonstrate

from Poland, as the name may suggest, but from Prague itself at the start of the 19th century. The origin of the name of the dance – according the the Czechs – is quite simple. The word *půl* means half, and the polka is a dance in double

their newly acquired talents to their mothers, in the glorious surroundings of Prague's ballrooms. The event marks their entry into society, and it is a highlight in the social calendar both for parents and pupils.

Polka

Make no mistake about the origins of the word polka – the Czechs are very sensitive about the matter. This jewel in the crown of national heritage did not come

time. Many Czech composers have written scores for this swirling "pas de deux," the most renowned being the *Škoda lásky* composed by Jaromír Vejvoda (1902–1988),

which has become internationally famous under its American name *Beer Barrel Polka*. Literally translated, it means "love that has flown away."

The season

January to March marks the height of the ball season, but you'll find people enjoying a good dance all year round. Each profession has its own event, from firefighters to chimney sweeps. There is even a Snobs' Ball. The grandest balls usually take place at the Lucerna Palace (see p. 61), the Žofín Palace (see p. 51) and at the Municipal House (see p. 55). The best way to fully appreciate their importance in Prague life is to take part in one of these evenings. Try to meet a few of the locals who might invite you.

DANCE FEVER

It is usually in the month of February that the *maturitní ples* (graduation dance) takes place. It has become almost an initiation rite, with the nervous pupils obliged to ask the principal instructor to dance. The audience, made up of friends and family, shows its support by raining money on the dancers, which is gathered up by the participants. They carry large nets to help them do this most effectively, proving that learning to dance has its rewards.

Flavors
of Prague

Czech cooking has much in common with that of its Austrian and German neighbors. It is best described as "Central European," with its robust winter fare, using lots of beef, pork, cabbage and fresh cream. The word "light" does not spring to mind when describing it, but there are some specialties that are truly delicious and which you really should try.

Traditional food

You'll soon discover that the same standard dishes appear on almost all restaurant menus. The national dish is pork served with dumplings and sauerkraut (*vepřové, knedlíky a zeli*). Equally popular is the dish known as *svíčková na smetaně*, which is a pot-roasted fillet of beef in a rich creamy sauce with a cranberry garnish. Hungarian *guláš* has found its second home here in Prague.

You should enjoy this beef stew, with its very generous onion and paprika sauce.

Polévka

A typical Prague meal starts with a simple soup known as *polévka*. It can be potato soup (*bramboračka*), mushroom soup (*houbová*), or a beef and potato soup (*gulášová*). The true gourmet will enjoy chopped tripe soup (*dršťková*) sometimes generously spiced

with paprika. A word of warning – always insist on your soup being served hot (*teplá*). There is a tendency for it to be brought to the table lukewarm.

Knedlíky

Although dumplings are German in origin and name they play a very important role

in Bohemian cooking. They are a specialty in many restaurants, but don't expect them to be like English dumplings. They resemble heavy white bread, and sliced dumplings accompany most hot dishes. They can be made with flour (*houskové*), grated potato and flour (*bramborové*) or bacon (*špekové*). Do give them a try, and if you are feeling very adventurous, you could also order fruit dumplings (*ovocné knedlíky*). These are served as a dessert with melted butter, confectioners' sugar and poppy seeds.

Bread crumbs with everything!

Smažený is an important word in the Czech vocabulary. It means fried in bread crumbs, and you will read it on every menu in every restaurant as it

Pork products

The famous Prague ham (*pražská šunka*) is often served as an appetizer with whipped cream and horseradish (*plněná šunka*). A slightly more sophisticated dish is made of pork sausage, sliced and marinated (or drowned) in vinegar (*utopenec*). You can buy salamis, sausages and other pork products in the many pork butchers in the city center. The meat is delicious and low in fat, and it is

particularly tasty when accompanied by gherkins. Make sure you try it at least once during your stay in Prague.

Christmas carp

Traditionally, the locals buy carp a week before Christmas. It is the main dish eaten at the Christmas Eve celebrations. Street vendors set up their stands in the city with barrels of fish, from which the locals make their selection. They're kept alive until December 24, when they're prepared in a variety of ways including carp soup, followed by fillets of carp fried in bread crumbs and served with a potato salad. You'll find that winter salads are often pickled and in summer are composed of tomato, lettuce, cucumber and peppers with a simple dressing.

is the most common way of preparing food. You'll have a wide choice of breaded dishes, including cheese, escalopes, meatballs, cauliflower and carp. These dishes can be excellent if fried well. Breaded and fried pork steak (*vepřový řízek*) is served with hot potatoes and a salad garnish with a slice of lemon. Try the *bramborák*, a potato pancake with salami and marjoram.

EATING ON THE RUN

In Prague people don't spend much time over their meals. The locals tend to grab something to eat when they feel hungry and stop in a snack bar (*bufet*) or a grocery store (*lahůdky*) to try one of their open sandwiches (*chlebíčky*). Follow their example and choose from a selection of ham, salami, gherkins, cream cheese, horseradish or salad with mayonnaise. Another option is to try the street stands and have frankfurters (*párky*) or grilled sausages (*klobásy*) served with chunks of brown bread and mustard. Sausage stands are very common in Central Europe and the locals either eat standing up or take the sausages away to eat cold. If you're hungry late in the evening, head for a *bufet*. They stay open late but not always all night.

Practicalities

Getting around the city

By car

If you're spending a weekend in Prague, it isn't necessary to have a car. You can explore Prague on foot or by public transportation. To park, non-residents have a choice between ticket machine parking spaces and fee-charging parking lots. If you park in a residents only zone (blue lines), you may come back to find your vehicle immobilized by a *botička* (clamp/Denver boot).

FINDING YOUR WAY

You'll find route maps for all the walks in this chapter at the head of each tour, and references to the main sights listed in the Don't Miss section.

If this happens, call the phone number on the document left on your windshield or call the police. The fine will be at least Kč700. You are strongly advised to park in the monitored parking lots, for example in Charles Square, where it will cost Kč40, or at one of the monitored parking lots at the edge of the city. Alternatively, try the underground parking lots on Národní Street, or by the main station. If you arrive in the Czech Republic by car, you must buy a windsheild sticker at the border: Kč100 for ten days, Kč200 for a month and Kč800 for a year. The sticker is sold in gas stations and post offices, and with it you are permitted to use the highways (for a year). The speed limit on highways is 130km per hour (81mph); in urban areas 50km per hour (31mph) and on country roads 90km per hour (56mph).

If you drive, you must not drink any alcohol. Breath tests are frequent, even in the center of the city and by law drivers are not permitted to have any alcohol in their blood.

By metro and tram

There are three lines on the subway. Line A is green and is the most useful for tourists. It covers all the main areas of the city center and crosses from east to west. Line B is yellow and C is red. The service in the city and in the suburbs is quite frequent, daily 5am to midnight. Tickets (*jízdenky*) can be bought at the automatic ticket machines in the metro stations, in street kiosks, in tobacco shops (*tabák*) or in hotels. Tickets are the same for both metro and trams but you must validate your ticket before your trip. Do this before taking the escalator into the subway and on entering a tram. An electronic message on trams will announce each stop and the one to follow, together with the connections for the metro. Night trams operate from midnight until 5am, and they have two-digit numbers, which always begin with 5. Timetables and tram maps are available at every stop, and the trams are remarkably punctual. Take a 22 tram from the center of Prague (Charles Square or Národní třída) to Prague Castle, crossing the Vltava and traveling via the Little Quarter (Malá Strana) – a scenic route.

How much does it cost?

Tickets cost Kč20 for 75 minutes with unlimited transfers and Kč14 for 20 minutes with no transfers. There is a reduced rate for under 15s (Kč7 and Kč10). The tickets are valid for 90 minutes from 8pm to 5am all week. You can also buy a network ticket: Kč120 for 24 hours, Kč220 for three days, Kč280 for seven days and Kč320 for 15 days. These tickets, together with maps of the city, metro and tram systems, are available from information centers and at automatic ticket machines in metro stations, including:

Palace on Masarykovo nábřeží. After a long walk around the city, you can also relax on a sunny day with a more leisurely trip aboard a boat along the Vltava river. An hour's trip costs around Kč170 and includes a drink. Choose from those on the Na Františku quay near the Čechův most bridge. It is better to choose a small boat rather than a huge tourist-packed one. If you are looking for a longer trip outside Prague itself, then go to the pier on Rašínovo nábřeží, Prague 2 (☎ 224 930 017, ☎ 224 913 862; www.paroplavba.cz). From there you can take a tour of the Trója Palace (1 hour) or the Slapy dam (4 hour).

The funicular

Using your tram and train ticket, you can take the funicular up the wooded hill of Petřín and on to the station at Štefánikova Hvězdárna, the Observatory. From the top of the hill, the view is magnificent, and you can enjoy a lovely walk in the forest on the top of the hill before returning to the city by the same route. Access to the funicular is at Újezd, 36, in the Malá Strana.

Muzeum station (every day 7am–9pm) and Můstek station (beneath Jungmannovo Square, Mon.-Fri. 8am–6pm; for both stations, ☎ 296 191 817), as well as the airport (every day 7am–10pm, ☎ 220 115 404, www.dpp.cz). The staff speak English.

By boat

An alternative way to travel, which is quieter but more strenuous, is by rowboat or pedal boat. You can rent them on Slavic Island for one or two hours. Go to the front of Žofín

Car rental

Having spent a weekend in Prague, you may feel tempted to explore outside the city. The most practical way is to rent a car. Take your driver's license and passport, and you can rent a Škoda Fabia or Octavia for about Kč1,500–2,200 per day. Contact one of the following.

Central Rent A Car
Černá Růže, Na Příkopě 12
Metro Dejvická
☎ 222 245 905.

Hertz

Karlovo náměstí 28, Prague 2
Metro Karlovo náměstí
☎ 222 23 10 10
www.hertz.cz

A-Rent Car

Washingtonova 9, Prague 1
Metro Muzeum
☎ 224 233 265
V celcini 10 (Millenium Plazza)
☎ 224 21 15 87
www.arentcar.cz

Europcar

Pařížská 28
☎ 224 811 290
www.europcar.cz

Making a telephone call

There are many public phones
in the city and in the metro
stations. It's best to use
phonecard telephones rather
than coin-operated ones,
which are very rarely working.
Buy a phonecard from one of
the newsstands (try Wenceslas
Square), a tobacco shop
(tábak), a post office or a
shop. Cards are available
from Kč200.

For calls to the UK from
Prague, dial 00 44; to Ireland
dial 00 353; to Australia
00 61; to New Zealand 00 64;
to the USA and Canada
dial 00 1. For calls to Prague
from the UK and Ireland
dial 00 420; from the USA
and Canada dial 011 420;
and from Australia and
New Zealand, dial 00 11 420.
Information has English-
speaking operators: ☎ 1180.
To call a number within Prague
dial only the nine-figure

telephone number beginning
with 2.
Avoid making telephone calls
from your hotel as you will
incur a heavy surcharge. The
dial tone is a short note and
then a long one. Long regular
notes indicate the ring tone
whereas the busy signal is a
series of short rapid notes.

Mailing a letter

You can buy stamps (poštovní
známka) with your postcards or
at the post office. Mailboxes
are easily recognizable and are
bright orange. The Main Post
Office (Hlavní pošta) is at
Václavské náměstí
(Jindřišská 14, Prague 1
☎ 221 13 11 11, 7am-8pm).
It's pretty large, so you
shouldn't miss it, and is open
24 hours a day, with a reduced
service at night. You can send
and receive faxes from here
on ☎ (00 420 2) 223 20 837.
There's another post office in
the Old Town, near metro
Staroměstská (Kaprova 12,
Prague 1).

Changing money

Don't even contemplate
exchanging money on

the black market on the streets
of Prague – you will almost
certainly be conned, and many
of these crooks have serious-
looking bodyguards. Use the
banks or the bureaux de
change, which stay open fairly
late (although watch the rates
in the exchange booths in
touristy areas – they really hike
the rates if you change small
amounts). You can also
withdraw cash at ATM
machines, which accept debit
and all major credit cards.

American Express

Václavské náměstí 56
☎ 222 80 01 11
Oct.-Apr.: Mon.-Fri. 9am-5pm,
Sat. 9am-noon; May-Sep.:
Mon.-Fri. 9am-6pm, Sat.
9am-2pm.

Komerční banka

Na příkopě 33
☎ 222 411 111
Mon.-Fri. 8-11am and 1-6pm.

Československá Obchodní banka

Na příkopě 14
Mon.-Fri. 7.30am-noon and
1-3.30pm.

EMBASSIES

American Embassy
Tržiště 15, Prague 1
☎ 257 320 663

Canadian Embassy
Mickiewiczova 6, Prague 1
☎ 272 101 800

British Embassy
Thunovská 14, Prague 1
☎ 257 530 278
www.britain.cz

Irish Embassy
Tržiště 13, Prague 1
☎ 257 530 061

Australian Consul
Na Ořechovce 38, Prague 6
☎ 224 31 07 43

New Zealand Consul
☎ 225 41 98
(for emergency use only).

Western Union
Jungmannova 31
☎ 224 494 346
Mon.-Fri. 10am-6pm.

Živnostenská Banka
Na příkopě 20
☎ 224 12 11 11
Mon.-Fri. 8.30am-5pm.

The 24-hour exchange desk at the airport is run by the Československá Obchodní banka.

Tourist Offices

Pražská Informační Služba
(P.I.S.)
Na příkopě 20
☎ 124 44
Mon.-Fri. 9am-6pm or 7pm,
Sat.-Sun. 9am-3.30pm or 5pm
www.pis.cz
The P.I.S. is a valuable and reliable source for detailed information and maps as well as various programs of cultural events.

Čedok
Na příkopě 18
Mon.-Fri. 9am-7pm,

Sat. 10am-3pm
☎ 800 112 112 / 224 197 106.
This is a useful place for general information, train and bus timetables and international tickets. Credit cards are accepted.

Opening hours

Museums and galleries are generally open from 9 or 10am until 5 or 6pm every day except Monday. Entrance charges are usually between Kč60 and Kč100. Churches are sometimes closed outside service hours; some have a limited access through the main gate only. Some charge an entrance fee. In the Jewish quarter, the synagogues and stores are closed on Saturdays. Tourists have to pay an entry charge of Kč500 for the cemetery and synagogue, but students will get a reduction on presentation of their student ID card.

USEFUL ADDRESSES

Velvet Voyages
This company will cater for all your needs as a tourist. They can arrange hotel reservations, guided tours, concert tickets, visits to crystal factories, even wine and beer tastings. Although originally set up to cater to French tourists, they also speak English and are generally very helpful.

Dobrovského, 10
☎ 233 373 376; 🖷 233 375 297
www.velvetvoyages.com
Email: velvetvoyages@mbox.vol.cz

CoDan Agentura
Based in Prague but covering the whole country, very efficient, CoDan Agentura can reserve hotel rooms, concert tickets and guided tours, etc. for groups and individuals.

Zlatnická 10, P.O. Box, 38, 110 00 Prague, 1
☎ 251 019 360; 🖷 251 019 361
www.andel3w.dk
Email: andel3w@bohem-net.cz

What to see in Prague
and sights not to miss

To help you discover the town, we have put together 11 walks through Prague, all illustrated by a map. If you only have a little time, here is a selection of 12 sights that you should absolutely try and see. They are all mentioned throughout this guidebook and you will also find more details about them at the end of the What to see section.

Museum of Modern and Contemporary Art

What was once a center for international trade fairs has now become home to a large number of masterpieces. Don't miss the self-portraits of Picasso and Douanier Rousseau.

Don't Miss, p. 68.

Museum of Decorative Arts

Only a small part of the museum's extraordinarily wealthy collections is exhibited, focusing on the arts and crafts of Bohemia and other regions of Central Europe, and on the art of Bohemian glass since the Middle Ages.

See walk no. 5, p. 51
and Don't Miss, p. 69.

Mucha Museum

Personal belongings, drawings, lithographs, theater posters: a journey into Mucha's art nouveau universe, which successfully merged his Slav heritage with a style which he developed in Paris.

See walk no. 9, p. 61
and Don't Miss, p. 70.

Municipal House

Large reception rooms, exhibition spaces, a coffee shop, two restaurants and Prague's largest concert hall (with 1,500 seats) make the Municipal House a Prague institution.

See walk no. 6, p. 55
and Don't Miss, p. 71.

Church of Our Lady before Týn

Located in the heart of the old city, you can't miss the two huge spires of Our Lady before Týn, famous for having been Prague's first Hussite church.

See walk no. 7, p. 57
and Don't Miss, p. 72.

St Vitus Cathedral

The cathedral is the country's largest religious sanctuary – its size and the treasures it contains are very impressive. The Mucha stained-glass window is exceptionally beautiful.

See walk no. 1, p. 36
and Don't Miss, p. 73.

Nerudova Street

Take your time to stroll down this street, full of tiny bourgeois houses and magnificent Baroque palaces. Look up to see fine examples of Prague's famous street signs: violins, eagles, the sun, etc. Jan Neruda, who gave the street its name, lived at no. 44 and at no. 47.

See walk no. 4, 46
and Don't Miss, p. 77.

Vyšehrad Cemetery

The most famous cemetery in Prague, and a national landmark. Dvořák, Mucha, Smetana and many others are buried here. The extravagant tomb stones were all made by local artists.

See walk no. 11, p. 66
and Don't Miss, p. 78.

St Nicholas of Malá Strana Church

The jewel of Prague Baroque architecture and the masterpiece of the Dientzenhofer family, the church is also blessed with exceptional acoustics. It hosts regular concert performances.

See walk no. 4, p. 46
and Don't Miss, p. 74.

Strahov Convent Library

The library contains nearly a million books. It was the two rooms of Philosophy and Theology which originally established the reputation of the Strahov monastery. It is the largest Romanesque construction in Bohemia.

See walk no. 2, p. 41
and Don't Miss, p. 75.

Charles Bridge

It's difficult to miss Charles Bridge. We suggest you cross the bridge at dusk, to better appreciate its magical atmosphere, its beautiful Baroque statues (*St John Nepomucene* by Brokof and *Saint Luitgarde* by Braun) and the beautiful view of the castle.

See walk no. 5, p. 50
and Don't Miss, p. 76.

The Old-New Synagogue

The last example of a European medieval synagogue, this is the oldest building in the old ghetto. Admire its stark style and its prayer room which encourages contemplation.

See walk no. 8, p. 59
and Don't Miss, p. 79.

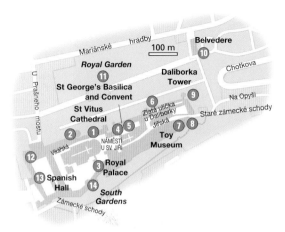

Mariánské hradby

Royal Garden

11 St George's Basilica and Convent

St Vitus Cathedral

Daliborka Tower

Belvedere **10**

Chotkova

Na Opyši

6 Zlatá ulička u Daliborky
Jiřská

9

Staré zámecké schody

2 **1** **4** **5**

7 **8**

Toy Museum

NÁMĚSTÍ U SV. JIŘÍ

Vikářská

12

3 Royal Palace

13 Spanish Hall

14 South Gardens

Zámecké schody

100 m

U Prašného mostu

Prague Castle,
a town within a town

From its picturesque vantage point, Prague Castle dominates the city. Originally the home of the Bohemian monarchy, the presidents of the Republic also lived here until Václav Havel chose a less ostentatious home. Soldiers parade proudly at noon every day to the sound of trumpets. Take a close look at their uniforms with their gold buttons. They were designed by Teodor Pištěk, costume designer to Miloš Forman, the film director. For those of you just wanting to relax, there are several cafés and restaurants within the castle precincts.

❶ St Vitus Cathedral★★★

Second courtyard
See Don't Miss, p. 73.

The French architect Matthew of Arras began work on the mighty Gothic cathedral in 1344, but it was not completed until 1929. The Rococo tomb of St John Nepomuk was crafted from two tons of solid silver in 1736. The magnificent art nouveau stained-glass window by Alphonse Mucha features St Cyril and St Methodius. Be

sure to visit St Wenceslas Chapel, where the walls are

decorated with polished semi-precious stones from Bohemia.

❷ Powder Tower

Built in the 16th century on the site of a defense stronghold, this sober tower overlooks the Deer Moat. First used as a workshop for the founder Tomas Jaros, then as an alchemist's laboratory during the reign of Rudolph II, it was converted to an ammunition depot in the 17th century. Today it houses a museum with

exhibits and displays connected with the art of foundry.

❸ The Royal Palace ★★★

Third courtyard.

Fortified in the 11th century, the oldest part of the Castle was inhabited by Czech kings until the Hapsburgs established their residency in Vienna in the 17th century. Designed at the end of the 15th century by Benedikt Riedl, the Vladislas Room is a real gem of Gothic architecture which will surprise with its monumental proportions. Also known as the Tournaments Room, knights and their horses used to gain access to it up the Knights staircase, capped with Gothic vaults and just as impressive. Through the Vladislas Room, you gain access to the Bohemian

Chancery where, on May 23, 1618, the infamous Defenestration of Prague took place, which was to be a prelude to the Thirty Years' War.

❹ St George's Basilica ★★

Third courtyard.

Flanked by its two white towers, this 10th-century Romanesque basilica is one of the best-preserved in the country. Altered several times, it has

been hiding since the 17th century behind a Baroque facade. Its harmonious interior is a perfect showcase for the tombs of the Premyslids, the first Bohemian sovereigns.

❺ St George's Convent ★★

Jiřské nám. 33 (third courtyard)
Every day except Mon. 10am-6pm
Tickets available on site (Kč100).

Established in 973 by Boleslas II, St George's Convent is the oldest convent in Bohemia and houses a very beautiful collection of Czech artwork.

The permanent collection, displayed on the second floor, comprises, among others, mannerist artworks from the time of Rudolph II, as well as Baroque paintings and sculptures by Matyas Braun, Karel Skréta and Petr Brandl.

ROCK AND ROLL

Bizarrely enough, the magnificent Spanish Hall (see p. 39) built in the 17th century has good reason to thank a very unlikely and modern benefactor in the form of one of the West's longest-lived and best-known rock groups. During their 1995 tour *The Rolling Stones* brought their considerable entourage to Prague and played to a huge crowd of more than 100,000 people. Afterward the group donated a large sum of money to the city to pay for the installation of a new lighting system in the Spanish Hall. As a result of their generous donation, its beams, chandeliers and trompe l'oeil murals are now illuminated to great effect. It is only a pity that few are able to see it for themselves now that the hall is closed to the general public.

❻ Golden Lane★★★
Zlatá Ulička
Entrance charge.

It is claimed that Emperor Rudolph II housed his alchemists in the tiny multi-colored cottages which were built into the walls of the Gothic fortifications. The shops in these tiny premises make their own pots of gold today by selling locally made crafts and souvenirs of all kinds. Kafka lived in no. 22 from 1917 to 1918, and he remains one of the street's most famous inhabitants.

❼ Toy Museum★★
Jiřská 6
☎ 224 372 294
Every day 9.30am-5.30pm.

Having created the Munich Toy Museum, Ivan Šteiger returned from exile in Germany to build a museum for Prague, telling the story of toys for the past 150 years. In its seven magical rooms you'll find miniature trains, tin toys, old stuffed bears, dollhouses and doll furniture and hundreds of Barbie dolls.

❽ Lobkowicz Palace Café★
Jiřská 3
☎ 602 595 998
Every day 10am-6pm.

Located opposite the Toy Museum, this 16th-century palace was returned to the Lobkowicz family in 2003. Apart from an elegant restaurant, it also boasts a large café

(sandwiches, salads, ice creams and pastries) with terraces from where you'll be able to admire a magnificent view over Prague. Concerts are held throughout the year at 1pm in the music room of the palace.

❾ Daliborka Tower★
The tower was used as a prison until 1781 and bears the name of its first inmate, Dalibor of Kozojedy, later immortalized in Smetana's opera. The citizens of Prague demanded his release, moved by his skill as a violinist. However, the prisoner did not manage to escape his fate and was beheaded in 1498.

❿ Belvedere★★
Královská zahrada.

Ferdinand I built this lovely summer house for his beloved wife Anne. You can just

picture the receptions and balls given in her honor. It's a fine Italian Renaissance building, built by Paolo della Stella and completed in 1564. Don't miss the *Singing Fountain* (1568), which owes its name to the musical sound the water makes as it hits the bronze bowl.

⓫ Royal Garden★★
Královská zahrada
Apr.-Oct. every day 10am-6pm
Entrance free.

Not to be confused with the South Gardens, the Royal Garden was designed according to Renaissance principles for Ferdinand I in 1535. The tulips that bloom in the spring are a distant echo of those the Emperor had brought back from Turkey by his ambassadors. He was the first to grow the flowers in

Europe, despite the harsh winters in Bohemia.

⓬ Na Baště★

Left of the entrance to the castle (Hrdčanske náměstí)
☎ 224 373 599
Every day 10am-6pm.

Nestling in this peaceful garden on the bastion (Na Baště), behind a small yew-lined terrace, this restaurant with its simple but bright decor offers light meals, drinks, pastries and ice creams. It has the advantage of being a little off the beaten track popular with tourists, but also boasts a small pleasantly shaded terrace opposite one of the elegant porticoes of the castle. It can also be reached via the north gate, by climbing some steps on the right before entering the castle.

⓭ The Spanish Hall★★

Second courtyard
Closed to the public.

The Central Committee of the Communist Party met for many years beneath the gilded chandeliers of this hall before it became a reception room for prestigious events. Sadly, it is out of bounds to the public, but concerts are occasionally held in this stunning room.

⓮ South Gardens★

Jižní zahrady
Apr.-Oct. every day 10am-6pm
Entrance free.

As a gesture of democracy, President Havel reopened these charming small gardens in 1990. They are located on the ramparts of the Castle and offer an uninterrupted view over the Old Royal Palace and the rooftops of the Little Quarter. There are two obelisks, which mark the spot where two governors, thrown from a window on one of the upper floors, landed safely during the Defenestration of 1618. This marked the prelude to the Thirty Years' War.

PRAGUE CASTLE, VISITOR'S CHECKLIST

The grounds in front of the castle are open to the public every day from 5am to midnight from April to October and from 6am to 11pm from November to March. The changing of the guard takes place with a fanfare at noon. The castle buildings are open every day from 9am to 5pm from April to October and from 9am to 4pm from November to March; gardens open every day from 10am to 6pm from April to October (only the garden on "the bastion" and the riding school ring terrace are open in winter). Tickets, valid for two days, are only sold in the information center located in the third courtyard. They will enable you to visit all the areas open to the public by choosing from four options (option A enables you to visit all of the castle, i.e. St Vitus Cathedral, the Royal Palace, St George's Basilica, the Powder Tower and Golden Lane). Audioguides in English are also available (☎ 777 200 202).

☎ 224 373 368 or 224 372 434; www.hrad.cz

Upper Hradčany

The third of Prague's five towns, Hradčany, was founded around 1320. A terrible fire destroyed the medieval district in 1541, so much of the area was then rebuilt, but little has changed since and Hradčany looks down from its high ground over the city much as it did centuries ago. Go at the end of the day to the gardens of Strahov Monastery to see Prague lit up by the rays of the setting sun.

❶ The Loretto★★★

Loretánské nám. 7
Tue.-Sun. 9am-12.15pm
and 1-4.30pm
☎ 220 516 740
Entrance charge.

Built in the 17th century to

house a replica of the Santa Casa (the house in Nazareth where the Annunciation is said to have taken place, moved in the 12th century by angels to Loretto in Italy), this sumptuous

Baroque sanctuary was finely carved by Kryštof and Kilian Dientzenhofer (1720–23). The interior of the Nativity Church exudes elegance and harmony. On the second floor, the Treasure Room houses the "sun of Prague," a monstrance composed of 6,222 diamonds piously donated in 1699 by countess Ludmila of Kolovrat.

❷ U černého vola★★

Loretánské nám. 1
☎ 220 513 481
Every day 10am-10pm.

Right next to the Loretto Church, this beautiful Baroque dwelling houses a small inn unknown to many tourists. In a relaxed and comfortable atmosphere, you'll be able to enjoy simple dishes at long wooden tables washed down with *Velkopopovický Kozel* beer.

4 Pohorelec Antiques

Pohorelec 9
☎ 220.514.287
Every day 9am-6pm.

In one of the oldest districts of Prague, on a large square surrounded by Baroque and Rococo buildings, this antique dealer is easy to find thanks to his beautiful shop sign. Inside, you'll discover a large range of religious icons, old coins and instruments. Some of the violins, made in Prague or Vienna, are signed and date back to the 18th century.

5 The Strahov Monastery★★★

Strahovské nádvoří 1
Every day 9am-noon and 1-5pm
Entrance charge
See Don't Miss, p. 75.

This monastery was founded in 1140 by a French religious order, the Premonstratensians, and they remained here, except for an enforced eviction during the Communist period. Make a point of visiting

the impressive libraries. Look around the Theology Room (1679) with its extensive stucco and its wall paintings, and visit the Philosophy Room (1782), named in tribute to the Age of Enlightenment.

6 Peklo★

("Hell")
Strahovské nádvoří
☎ 220 51 66 52
Every day 11am-midnight.

Despite its rather alarming name, you can enter without fear into this restaurant in the old cellars of Strahov Monastery. There's a choice of Czech or Italian food but its location is more impressive than its menu. No doubt it was the monks who were responsible for naming this place of temptation.

7 U Zavěšenýho Kafe★

Úvoz 6
☎ 605 294 595
Every day 11am-midnight.

In his tiny café, Jakub Krejí is able to display his works on the

8 ČERNÍN PALACE★★

Having quarreled with Bernini, Count Černín commissioned Francesco Caratti to complete the 150m (500ft) facade, decorated with 30 Palladian half-columns. It was finally finished three centuries later (1669–1936). Just days after the Communist coup in 1948, Jan Masaryk, popular son of Czechoslovakia's first president, Tomáš Masaryk, fell to his death from one of the windows of the Ministry of Foreign Affairs.

Loretánské nám.; closed to the public.

wall and serve large beers to customers sitting on long wooden tables. It's like a mountain chalet inside. If you are feeling brave, try the *pivní sýr* (cheese with beer) or the *nakládaný hermelín* (marinated camembert). These are house specialties with very powerful flavors.

❽ Marionety

Nerudova 51
☎ 257 533 035
Every day 10am-6pm.

Fashioned from wood, resin and ceramics, the puppets on display here have all been made according to traditional Czech craftsmanship. Always very expressive, their finish is impeccable and they can be quite large. Animals verging on the extraordinary can be found next to fairy-tale characters, not forgetting the ubiquitous witches.

❾ Allure4u★

Nerudova 24
☎ 602 696 128
Every day 10am-7pm.

This shop is for amateurs of glass and crystalware seeking rare originals as well as modern imitations. You'll find everything here from antiques to modern handmade replicas: glasses, lamps, jewelry in a variety of styles, from Renaissance, Secession and art nouveau to contemporary. Glasses start at Kč1,500, lamps at Kč16,000. There is the possibility of organizing a visit to a glass-blowing workshop by special request.

❿ Schwarzenberg Palace★

Hradčanské nám. 2
Closed for restoration.

Built between 1555 and 1576 in the Florentine style, this vast Renaissance-style palace is home to the collections of the military museum (due to reopen in 2007). From a distance, its majestic facade appears to be embossed with diamond points, but in reality this is an optical illusion created by

superb sgraffiti. Although it was altered during the Baroque period, a large part of the original decoration remains intact.

⓫ Hradčanské náměstí★★

This square commands the most prestigious position, much prized by Czech nobility. The Lobkowicz, Schwarzen-berg, Thun-Hohenstein, Martinic and Sternberg families competed to outdo each other, as the various places bearing their names testify. Alphonse Mucha (see p. 14) lived in the Baroque house at no. 6, where part of Miloš Forman's film *Amadeus* was set.

⓬ Šternberg Palace★★

Hradčanské nám. 15
☎ 220 514 634
Tue.-Sun. 10am-6pm
Entrance charge.

Count Šternberg donated this Baroque palace to the Society of Patriotic Friends of the Arts

in Bohemia, which he founded in 1796. The palace houses a selection of works from the Italian, Flemish and German schools of the 15th to 18th centuries. Don't miss The *Feast of the Rosary* by Dürer (1506). Emperor Rudolph II ordered that the painting be brought from Venice on a man's back.

⑬ U Zlaté hrušky (The Golden Pear)★★

Nový Svět 3
☎ 220 51 47 78
Every day 11.30am-1pm.

Dishes such as venison in red wine and duck with honey and almonds are on the menu at this restaurant which specializes in game, located in a 16th-century house. You can eat in the garden in summer,

and you'll enjoy excellent Czech dishes. The cuisine by a Czech chef is exquisite. Read the prices on the menu carefully and look closely at the check. This is the heart of the tourist area: Less than scrupulous hosts could be tempted to take advantage of you. Reservations essential.

⑮ Nový Svět street★

Here you'll see a totally different scale of living from that of Hradčany Square. To make it clear that they were not ashamed of their poverty, the 14th-century castle workers gave their humble cottages golden house signs shaped like pears, grapes, bushes and acorns. The houses are now being renovated, and no doubt

prices in this charming area will soon escalate.

⑯ U Raka Pension★★

Černínská 10
☎ 220 51 11 00
❻ 233 358 041.

Here's a bit of countryside in the heart of the city. This half-timbered cottage dates from the end of the 18th century and has six lovely rooms. It's the perfect hideout, and does not allow children or dogs. You can just enjoy a cup of tea or a glass of Moravian wine, if the accommodations are beyond your budget. Ring the bell and you'll be greeted by a cheerful host (every day 2-7pm, cold dishes).

⑭ NOVÝ SVĚT GALLERY★★

Jana Reichová opened this renovated and dynamic gallery in 1994, celebrating the 300th anniversary of the Baroque building in which it is housed. In the basement (originally the coal cellar), there are regular exhibitions of the works of the best contemporary artists. On the first floor, under a fresco of St John Nepomuk, patron of Hradčany and canonized in 1729, you'll discover the photographs of Josef Sudek, glass pieces by Šípek and drawings and engravings by Theimer, Sopko and Sládek. There are beautiful art books and carefully selected copies of antique glasses, costing from just Kč100 up to as much as Kč200,000.

Nový Svět 5; ☎ 220 51 46 11
Every day 10am-6pm.

Vlašská
Vlašská
Tržiště
Vrtbovská Gardens
Kamelitská
St Mary the Victorious
Hellichova
Michna Palace
200 m
Strahovská
Hunger Wall
Petřín Park
Újezd
NÁMĚSTÍ KINSKÝCH
Holečkova

Petřín,
lovers' hill

If you're in a romantic mood, take a walk on the wooded slopes of Petřín Hill. The southern side was planted with vineyards in the 12th century, but by the 18th century these had been transformed into gardens and orchards. It's a perfect spot for a romantic stroll, and the local tradition is for lovers to embrace in front of the monument to Karel Hynek Mácha, the famous Czech Romantic poet, who died in 1836 at the age of 26.

scaled-down version of the Eiffel Tower, with 299 steps and no elevator. From the tower, weather permitting, you should

be able to see Bohemia's highest peak in the Giant Mountains, known as Sněžka.

❶ Petřín Park★★
Access by funicular, Újezd 17 Mar.-Aug. every day 10am-10pm; Sep.-Oct. every day 10am-6pm.

Jump on the funicular (U Lanová dráhy, Ujezd St.) and you'll soon find yourself on the rooftop of Prague. The Observation Tower and the Church of St Lawrence are at the summit, together with two relics from the 1891 Jubilee Exhibition. Try navigating the Mirror Maze and climbing the

❷ Hunger Wall★
The remains of almost 1,200m (1,300 yds) of crenellated fortifications run from Újezd to

Strahov across Petřín Park. Built in 1360–62, the wall takes its name from a decision made by Charles IV to order the construction of a huge wall as employment for the poor and wretched victims of a dreadful famine. The battlements are also said by some to resemble teeth.

❸ Vlašská Street★

The most picturesque way to descend from Petřín is to take the "Italian street," so called because of the immigrants who settled there to rebuild the Castle in the 16th century. The grandest building is Lobkowicz Palace, now the German embassy. It is one of the finest Baroque palaces, built by the Italian Alliprandi at the beginning of the 18th century. It is best viewed from the rear but sadly the magnificent gardens are no longer open to the public.

❹ Vrtbovská Gardens★★

(Vrtbovská zahrada)
Karmelitská 25
☎ 257 53 14 80
Apr.-Oct. every day 10am-6pm;
May-Sep. every day 10am-7pm
Classical concerts every day
at 6.30pm
Entrance charge.

This beautiful Baroque garden lies behind Vrtbov Palace and has magnificent views. The statues of classical gods and stone vases were sculpted by Matthias Braun, while the garden itself was designed by Franktišek Maximilián Kaňka in about 1720.

❻ V Karmelitské★

Karmelitská 20
☎ 257 535 152
Mon.-Fri. 7am-7pm, Sat.
10am-7pm, Sun. 10am-10pm.

This baker, pastry shop and

❺ CHURCH OF ST MARY THE VICTORIOUS★★

Prague's first Baroque church houses the *Bambino di Praga*, a wax effigy of the infant Jesus brought from Spain in the 15th century and attributed with miraculous powers. The effigy has an extensive wardrobe, which comprises over 60 different coats. One of the coats was sewn by Maria Theresa of Austria herself in gratitude for protecting the city during the French occupation in 1742. The effigy also has a record of miracle cures.

Karmelitská 9
Every day 8.30am-7pm.

tearoom with its slightly outdated atmosphere is the ideal place to take a break between two visits and to enjoy a pastry (the *jablkový závin* – apfelstrudel – is delicious) or an ice cream. Nearby, you can admire the elegant facade of the Baroque Michna Palace (Újezd, 40), the former summer residence of the Kinský family.

❼ Nebozízek Restaurant ★★

Petřínské Sady 411

☎ 257 315 329
Every day 11am-11pm.

This restaurant is worth a detour for its unbeatable view. It takes its name from the winding path up the hill which you take to reach it. Alternatively, you can walk from the funicular station halfway up the hill. The view is much more spectacular than the food.

Malá Strana,
the aristocratic "Little Quarter"

Malá Strana was founded in the 13th century on the slopes below the Castle. It reached the height of its splendor when the Catholic nobility built their sumptuous palaces there after the Battle of the White Mountain in 1620. You'll see many fine buildings, some of which are now foreign embassies. The area has retained much of its traditional character. To enjoy the romantic atmosphere, wander along the narrow cobbled streets and then relax in one of the many cafés on Nerudova street.

❶ Malostranské náměstí★★
Little Quarter Square.

The houses around the square (founded in 1257) were originally built in the Middle Ages but rebuilt in the Renaissance and the Baroque periods. The square divides around the Church of St Nicholas and in its center is a column which marks the end of a plague epidemic in 1713.

❷ Nerudova Street★★
See Don't Miss, p. 77.
This street is named after the 19th-century writer Jan

Neruda, author of many short stories set in this part of Prague. He lived in the houses called *The Two Suns* (no. 47) and *The Three Black Eagles*

(no. 44). Look out for the Morzin Palace (no. 5, the Romanian embassy), which has two massive statues of Moors (a pun on the owner's name). These were the work of the sculptor Ferdinand Maximilián Brokof. The Thun-Hohenstein Palace (no. 20, now the Italian embassy) is a grand Baroque building.

❸ Church of St Nicholas★★★
Malostranské nám.
☎ 257 534 215
Apr.-Sep. 9am-5pm, Oct.-Mar. 9am-4.30pm; bell tower: Apr.-Oct. 10am-4pm
Entrance charge
See Don't Miss, p. 74.

This church, a family masterpiece, is the most magnificent Jesuit-influenced Baroque building in the city. Krystof Dientzenhofer began work on it in 1703, followed by his son Kilian Ignaz, and Kilian's son-in-law, Anselmo

Lugaro, completed the building in 1755. You'll get the best view of the statues, frescoes and paintings by going to one of the concerts. Mozart himself played the organ in the church in 1787.

❹ Church of St Thomas★★

Josefská 8
☎ 257 530 556
Visit during services:
Mon.-Fri. 12.15am and 7pm;
Sat. 6pm; Sun. 9.30am, 11am,
12.30am and 6pm.

Kilian Ignaz Dientzenhofer was also responsible for this church, but this time on his own. It was built to replace a Gothic church destroyed in the Hussite wars. The two Rubens above the altar are copies. The originals are in the National Gallery, now housed in Prague's Sternberg Palace.

❺ St Thomas's Brewery★

Letenská 12
☎ 257 531 835
Every day 11.30am-11pm.

The Augustinian monks first brewed beer at St Thomas's in 1352. It was such a tasty brew that they became sole purveyor to Prague Castle. There are three beer halls in the basement, where you can now enjoy a dark beer from the Braník brewery.

❻ Wallenstein Palace and Garden★★

Valdštejnské nám. 4
Riding school Tue.-Sun.
9am-6pm; Garden May-Sep.
every day 9am-7pm.

This early Baroque palace was built in 1624–30 for Count Albrecht of Wallenstein. Over 30 houses, three churches and the municipal brick kiln were destroyed to make way for the building. Emperor Ferdinand II appointed Wallenstein as imperial military commander, and the latter had a portrait painted of himself as Mars on the ceiling of a palace room now used for state functions. The former riding school currently houses exhibitions by the National Gallery. There are copies of works by Adriaen de Vries, the originals having been stolen by the invading Swedes in 1648. On Saturday and Sunday from 10am to 6pm, certain rooms of the palace are open free to the public.

❼ Pálffy Palace Restaurant★★

Valdštejnská 14
☎ 257 530 522
Every day 11am-midnight.

This Baroque palace is home to the conservatoire of music and

a restaurant with a wonderful atmosphere. Dine by candle-light in beautiful surroundings with the most fashionable locals. The food is an unusual combination of Czech and Californian culinary styles!

❽ Ledebour Garden★★

Valdštejnská 3
Every day 10am-7.30pm
Entrance charge.

From the steps to the garden you'll be treated to a spectacular view of the rooftops of Prague. You can see into the hidden courtyards of the Little Quarter and behind its secret facades. The garden was designed in the 18th century and has a lovely pavilion. Three gardens

belonging to the former Ledebour, Černin and Pálffy palaces are linked together, and they have recently been restored. Enjoy the Tuscan-style balustraded terraces in this maze of a garden, and wander through the classical statues, old fountains and ornamental urns. Choose a pleasant spot by the vines and water plants to enjoy the superb view.

❿ Mostecka Ulice

(Bridge Street)
Linking Charles Bridge to the Small Side Square, this very touristy and generally packed street remains one of the prettiest in the old town. Lined with buildings from the Renaissance and Baroque

periods with brightly colored facades, it provides a delightful perspective with the church of St Nicholas in the background. Don't forget to look up and, if you ignore the surrounding stores, you'll discover charming scenes in the town where you least expect them.

⓫ Zlaty pstros★

Prokopska 5

☎ 728 026 973
Mon.-Fri. 11am-7pm,
Sat.-Sun. 1-6pm.

As soon as you get close to this small shop, a delicious scent of spices will waft up your nose. In a pretty vaulted room with a white ceiling, the wooden shelves and counter are laden with countless glass jars full of spices. Apart from the warm welcome, there are so many spices to choose from that you'll find it hard to resist. You can also find two delicious Moravian wines: *Frankovka* and *Svatovavrinnecké*.

⓬ U Vladaře★

Maltézské nám. 10
☎ 257 53 41 21
Every day noon-midnight.

On your left is a welcoming restaurant, which you'll no doubt be encouraged to try out. Be strong, resist and enter the tavern on the right instead.

Here you'll dine in an equestrian setting, complete with stagecoach lamps, and be served delicious Czech dishes. This is the perfect opportunity to try dumplings (*knedlíky*).

⑬ Maltézské nám★★
(Maltese Square)
Grand palaces surround this square, and several embassies seem to be competing for the prize of the most elegant. Nostitz Palace at no. 1, a majestic Baroque building? Straka Palace, which is plainer, at no. 14? Marvelous Turba Palace, in the Rococo style, occupied by Japan at no. 6? Or the Danish embassy at no. 5?

⑭ Buquoy Palace★★
Velkopřevorské nám. 2
Closed to the public.

The French embassy is located in a delightful Baroque building (1738), in which Miloš Forman filmed several of the scenes for his film *Amadeus*, which features numerous rooms from

the former home of the Buquoy family, originally from Flanders.

⑮ Kampa Island★★
Kampa is the largest of the islands in the Vltava and is formed by a branch of the river known as the Devil's Stream (*čertovka*). It's said to be haunted by evil spirits. There are three old mills on the island and the restored wheel of the Grand Prior's Mill. It has become known as the "Venice

of Prague," but with the occasional canoe instead of gondolas. It was once home to several artists, including the composer Bohuslav Martiný and the poet Vítězslav Nezval. The oval main square, Na Kampě, has some lovely 17th-century houses around it.

⑯ Kampa Museum★
U Sovových mlýnů 2
☎ 257 286 147
Tue.-Sun. 10am-6pm.

On the banks of the Vltava, just upstream from Charles Bridge, a real medieval mill has been adapted to provide a fitting space to display the works by the famous colorist František Kupka (1871–1957) and by a few other big names of contemporary art such as Otto Gutfreund and Jiří Kolář. With a wide view over the river, the restaurant next to the museum is worth stopping at.

⑨ TŘÍ PŠTROSŮ HOTEL★★
(The Three Ostriches)
The three ostriches on the front wall of the hotel were originally painted in the 17th century by Master Jan Fux, supplier of ostrich feathers to the court. The rooms are small, noisy and expensive. Do try and take a look at their painted wood Renaissance ceilings or at the exquisite ceiling in the small restaurant. Here you can enjoy a traditional meal in elegant surroundings. Choose from carp, goulash and a large selection of beef dishes.
Dražického nám. 12
☎ 257 288 888
Restaurant every day 11.30am-1am.

Beneath Charles
Bridge runs the Vltava

All roads lead to the medieval Charles Bridge, Prague's most familiar monument and home to numerous souvenir stalls. Its fame is due mostly to the 30 magnificent Baroque statues which line each side, though when first built its only decoration was a simple bronze crucifix. The River Vltava running beneath provides relief to the landlocked Czechs when they tire of city life and go in search of broader vistas.

Rudolfinum

3

4

J. PALACHA
NÁMĚSTÍ Museum of
Kaprova Decorative
Arts

Křížovnická

CHARLES
BRIDGE 2

KARLŮV KŘÍŽOVNICKÉ
MOST NÁMĚSTÍ
Karlova
1 Smetana
5 Museum

Smetanovo nábřeží Karoliny Divadelní Světlé

MOST Národní
LEGIÍ
200 m

Masarykovo nábřeží

6

Slovanský
ostrov

7 Mánes
Gallery

❶ Charles Bridge★★★

See Don't Miss, p. 76.
The bridge has connected the Malá Strana (Little Quarter) to the Staré Město (Old Town) since the 14th century, and it was the only crossing over the Vltava until the 18th century. Thousands of people use it daily, but there's no need to panic about its strength. According to legend, the builders mixed eggs with the mortar to strengthen it. Allow the magic of this spot to do its work, and run the gauntlet of the 30 statues at dawn or at dusk. It's an unforgettable experience.

❷ Národní Banka vín★★

Platnéřská 4
(entrance via Krizovnicka, 1)
☎ 221 10 82 44
Mon.-Fri. 10am-7pm,
Sat. 1-6pm.
In the cellars of St Francis Church is a "wine bank" for storing maturing wines, that has been blessed by the papal nuncio to the Czech Republic. Here you can select a good Moravian wine, with the benefit of Adéla Andráková's advice and knowledge, gained through her studies in France.

❸ Rudolfinum★

Nám. Jana Palacha 1
☎ 227 059 111
and 227 059 227.

This splendid example of neo-Renaissance architecture bears the name of the Austrian archduke, Rudolph of Hapsburg. It is now the home of the Czech Philharmonic Orchestra. Some of the most impressive concerts in the

Prague Spring music festival have been held in the sumptuous Dvořák Hall.

❹ Museum of Decorative Arts★

17 Listopadu 2
☎ 251 093 296
Tue.-Sun. 10am-6pm
Entrance charge
See Don't Miss, p. 69.

The museum has a unique collection of furniture, rugs, clocks and glass, which range in style from Renaissance to Biedermeier. The very best of Bohemian art is on display in one of the most fascinating museums in the city. There's an excellent café, which is the favorite haunt of students of the decorative arts.

❺ Smetana Museum★

Novotného lávka 1
☎ 222 220 082
Every day except
Tue. 10am-5pm.

A former neo-Renaissance waterworks has been converted into a memorial to Bedřich Smetana, and the museum is on a spit of land beside the river. This is an ideal location for the composer of *Vltava*, part of the cycle known as *Ma Vlast* (My Fatherland). The museum contains his piano together with scores and documents detailing the life of the most nationalist of great Czech composers.

❼ Mánes Gallery★

Masarykovo nábřeží 250
☎ 224 930 754
Tue.-Sun. 10am-6pm.

This white functionalist building was completed in 1932 and is named after Josef Mánes, a 19th-century landscape painter. This prestigious gallery regularly stages quality exhibits of contemporary artwork. There is also a café-restaurant with a terrace on the second floor from where you have an exceptional view over the river Vltava (☎ 224 931 112; every day 11am-11pm).

❻ GASTRO ŽOFÍN RESTAURANT★

This huge yellow building dominates the island known as Žofín, named after Sophie, mother of Emperor Franz Josef I. The island was the result of natural silting of the river in the 18th century. Lavish balls were held in the building at the end of the 19th century by the cream of Prague society, and concerts still take place today. In summer you can enjoy sitting in the outside area of this restaurant, which serves robust Czech food. If you're feeling romantic, rent a boat and row with your loved one down the river. Boats are available to rent from May through October.

Žofín 226
☎ 224 934 548
Every day 11am-midnight.

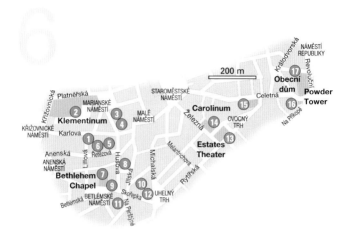

Staré Město,
the streets of the old town

As its name suggests, this is the oldest of the towns of Prague and the first to achieve this status and accompanying privileges in about 1230, when Prague found itself at the cross-roads of central European trade routes. Here the Prague of labyrinthine medieval passages and alleyways begins and many of its busiest restaurants and shops are to be found. You'll enjoy soaking up the atmosphere in these narrow old streets at the heart of the city.

❶ Karlova Street★★

This narrow, winding street dates back to the 12th century and links Charles Bridge and Old Town Square. Its many shops sell mainly souvenirs, glassware and wooden toys. Follow the Royal Route, along which kings and queens of Bohemia passed on their way to their coronation at St Vitus Cathedral. Watch out for the Renaissance building known as the "House of the Crown of

France" (no. 4), where Kepler drew up the laws bearing his name on the movement of planets between 1607 and 1612. Prague's first café was established in 1714 at the House of the Golden Snake (no. 18).

❷ Klementinum★★

Karlova 1
☎ 221 663 111
Mar.-Dec. Mon.-Fri. 10am-7pm.

This vast Baroque complex, the largest group of buildings

after the castle, was established in 1556 by the Jesuits to support emperor Ferdinand I in his policy of the restoration of the Catholic religion in Bohemia. You can now visit its splendid library adorned with frescoes, designed by K. I. Dienzenhofer at the beginning of the 18th century and the astronomy tower started in 1775. You can

also attend a concert in the superb chapel of mirrors adorned with stucco decorations.

❸ Clam-Gallas Palace

Husova 20
Only open for concerts.

Built between 1713 and 1730, this sumptuous Baroque palace is the work of the famous Austrian architect, Johann Bernhard Fischer von Erlach. Superbly restored, its grand staircase is enhanced by sculptures produced by Matyas Braun, who also created the majestic atlas statues which frame the gate.

❹ Mucha Museum Shop

Karlova 34
☎ 222 221 189
Every day 10am-6pm.

In this small shop at the corner of Karlova and Husova streets, you'll probably find a souvenir you wish to bring back home: postcard reproductions of the most famous paintings found in the Prague museums, posters, card games, jigsaw puzzles, notebooks or scarves, but also replicas of items, of art nouveau jewelry (brooches, necklaces and bracelets) inspired by Alphonse Mucha.

❺ U Zlatého tygra★★

Husova 17
☎ 222 22 11 11
Every day 3-11pm.

The "Golden Tiger" has become a bit of a cult pub, where the late writer Bohumil Hrabal came to find inspiration. He died in 1997 at the age of 83. Don't be intimidated by the predominantly male clientele, most of whom will be locals. They'll move up to fit you in at the long tables. Order a Pilsen and you'll be instantly accepted.

❻ House of the Lords of Kunštát★

Řetězová 3
Open in summer.

To avoid flooding, the level of this house has been raised, and in the basement there are three of Prague's best-preserved Romanesque rooms. The Lord of Kunštát offered his home to his nephew George of Poděbrady, future king of Bohemia, in the 15th century.

Another place you can go to marvel at constructions from the 12th century is the vaulted interior of the Fine Arts Museum (Husova 19, ☎ 222 220 218, Tue.-Sun. 10am-6pm).

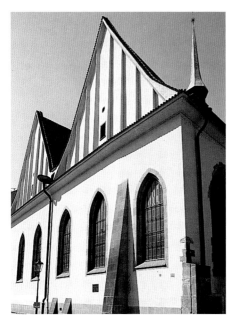

is always busy and only sells local produce from the Blatnicka cooperative in South Moravia. If you find yourself hesitating between a *Vavřinecké* and a *Riesling*, ask Zdeněk what he would suggest. His Moravian hospitality will transcend any language barriers that may exist.

⑪ Monarch

Na Perštýně 15
☎ 224 239 602
Bar: every day 3pm-midnight
Store: Mon.-Fri. 11am-7pm,
Sat. noon-6pm.

Don't hesitate to come and take a break in this modern and bright wine bar. Enjoy a good glass of wine while nibbling a piece of strong cheese. You'll find excellent vintages from all over the world and, if you feel like it, you can then go into the store to buy a bottle of your choice.

⑦ Bethlehem Chapel★

Betlémské nám. 4
☎ 224 248 595
Tue.-Sun. 10am-5.30pm
Entrance charge.

Although this chapel is a faithful reconstruction, completed by Jarosla Frágner after World War II, you'll be treading on the same ground as the famous reformer, Jan Hus. He delivered his passionate sermons against the Church and the Pope between 1402 and 1412. This is the place to visit if you're eager to learn more about the Hussites.

⑧ Church of St Giles

Husova 8
Open during services.

Founded at the end of the 13th century, this church has kept

its elegant Gothic gate. Altered by the Dominicans during the 18th century, the interior is essentially Baroque. The central nave boasts a fresco entitled *The Triumph of Dominicans over Heresy*.

⑨ Klub Architektů★

Betlémské nám. 5
☎ 224 40 12 14
Every day 11.30am-midnight.

This restaurant is run by the Institute of Architects and is a favorite haunt of artists and intellectuals. In the summer you can enjoy a candlelight meal on the terrace overlooking the Bethlehem Chapel. Reservations essential.

⑩ Vinárna Blatnička★

Michalská 5
Mon.-Fri. 10am-10pm.

This is a lively wine bar, which

⑫ Tesař Gallery★★

Skořepca 4
☎ 605 974 302
Mon.-Sat. 10am-7pm.

If you love crystal, it's worth stopping off at this small, sober but original gallery. You'll find delicate, elegantly designed creations of white cut crystal, representing excellent value for

money. An ideal place if you'd like to take back a carafe, glasses (for wine, vodka, tequila, etc.) or champagne glasses, sold by the piece or in sets of six. Everything is made by craftsmen but, unlike in the tourist shops, you won't find any colored glass here.

⑭ Carolinum★

Železná 9
☎ 224 49 16 32
Closed to the public.

Charles IV founded Central Europe's first university here in

1348, determined to make Prague the political and cultural center of Europe. Today this ancient Baroque building is the administrative core of the Charles University. It has a few beautiful Gothic touches, which are at their best when viewed from the corner of Železná and Ovocný trh.

⑮ Statue of the Black Virgin★★

Celetná 34
☎ 224 211 732
Every day except Mon.
10am-6pm.

Josef Gočár erected this controversial building in 1912. It was formerly a Baroque residence but only the symbolic statue of the Black Virgin remained after its reconstruction, hence its name

"House of the Black Virgin." You'll notice the statue, apparently locked up in a small cage, on one of the building's corners.

⑯ The Powder Tower★

Na příkopě
☎ 724 063 723
Apr.-Oct. every day 10am-6pm.

This tower acquired its name when it was used to store gunpowder in the 17th century. It is now a museum, housing exhibitions on Prague's towers.

Much more impressive, however, is the magnificent view over a sea of gray-green domes and tiled roofs which is well worth the climb up this vestige of the Old Town's few remaining ramparts.

⑰ Obecní dům★★★

(Municipal House)
Nám. Republiky 5
☎ 222 002 101
Every day 10am-6pm
See Don't Miss, p. 71.

This delightful art nouveau building, lovingly restored and a draw for enthusiasts of this style, was designed by Antonin Balšánek and Osvald Polívka (1905–1911). Works by Alphonse Mucha decorate the interior, alongside those of other leading Czech artists from the first decade of the 20th century. It houses a selection of venues: a French brasserie, a splendid Viennese-style café, the Plzeňská restaurant and the Smetana concert hall. There are tours in English nearly every day.

⑱ THE ESTATES THEATER★★

On October 29 1787, Mozart's *Don Giovanni* had its debut here with the composer himself at the piano. It was a historic performance, made even more remarkable by the fact that Mozart had composed his famous overture in D minor only two days before. The theater itself is one of the finest examples of neo-Classical architecture in Prague.

Stavoské divadlo; Ovocný trh 1
☎ 224 902 111
www.narodni-divadlo.cz

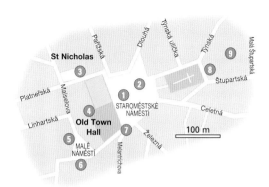

Staroměstské náměstí,
the Old Town Square

The Old Town Hall is one of Prague's most striking buildings. Originally established in 1338, it has expanded over the centuries and now consists of a row of colorful Gothic and Renaissance buildings. After serious damage by the Nazis in the 1945 Prague Uprising, most of these buildings were restored. The Old Town Square itself is the traditional heart of the city, full of cafés, stores and, of course, tourists.

❶ Staroměstské náměstí★★★
(Old Town Square)

This is the oldest market in the town, dating back to 1091, and is a perfect venue for an open-air lesson in Czech history. You'll see 27 white crosses set into the paving, which symbolize the Protestants executed in 1621 following the Battle of the White Mountain. It was after this that the country fell to the Hapsburgs. Klement Gottwald proclaimed the Communist state in the town square in 1948, and Václav Havel announced the return to democracy in the same square 42 years later.

❷ Jan Hus Monument ★
Ladislas Šaloun's art-nouveau monument to Jan Hus was unveiled on the 500th anniversary of the reformer's death. He was burned alive in 1415 after being pronounced a heretic. This massive symbol of national identity is also a popular meeting place.

❸ Church of St Nicholas★
Staroměstské nám. 27
☎ 224 190 991
Mon.-Sat. 10am-4pm,
Sun. noon-4pm
Entrance free.

The present church by Ignaz Dientzenhofer was completed in 1735, though there has been a church on this site since the 12th century. It looks rather like a wedding cake with its white facade studded with statues. Don't miss the enormous Bohemian chandelier.

❹ Old Town Hall★★★

Staroměstské nám. 1
☎ 236 002 562
Apr.-Oct. Mon. 11am-6pm,
Tue.-Sun. 9am-6pm;
Nov.-Mar. Mon. 11am-5pm,
Tue.-Sun. 9am-5pm
Entrance charge.

The astronomical clock (1410) is the town hall's main attraction. On the hour, a crowd of tourists and locals gathers to watch the procession of clock figures depicting Christ, followed by his apostles, while a skeleton pulls on the rope to ring a bell. To complete your visit, take the elevator up to the top of the tower (70m/230ft) to experience an exceptional view over the town, and don't forget to visit the Gothic room of the town council.

❻ Malé náměstí★★

(The Small Square)

Prague's first apothecary opened in 1353 on this delightful extension of the Old Town Square. The *Lékarná Schöblingová* (no. 13) has become a boutique but has

preserved its beautiful Baroque interior. Take a look and don't miss the superb Renaissance fountain on the square.

❼ Grand Café Praha★

Staroměstské nám. 22
☎ 221 632 520
Every day 8am-midnight.

On the second floor, the former *Milena* tearoom (named after Milena Jesenská, a friend of Franz Kafka) is today a modern café, which is more peaceful than the ones on the square.

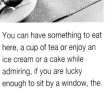

You can have something to eat here, a cup of tea or enjoy an ice cream or a cake while admiring, if you are lucky enough to sit by a window, the lovely view over the square.

❽ Church of Our Lady before Týn★★

Staroměstské nám. 14
☎ 224 213 475
Mon.-Fri. 9am-noon and 1-2pm;
services: Sat. 8am,
Sun. 9.30am and 9pm
See Don't Miss, p. 72.

This dark Gothic church (1365) was the most important of the Hussite churches built in Prague. Its steeples dominate the square, and it houses the tomb of the Danish astronomer Tycho Brahé, who died of a ruptured bladder during a royal audience with Rudolph II. Not wanting to "die like Tycho Brahé" is a colloquialism for needing to go to the bathroom.

❾ Týn Courtyard★★

This courtyard is better known by its German name *Ungelt*, meaning "no money," meant to deter invaders. Between the 11th and 18th centuries foreign merchants were housed here, and it became a successful international marketplace. The Granovský house, recognizable by its elegant second floor open loggia, was built in 1560 on the lines of an Italian Renaissance palace. Its sgraffito frescoes show scenes from the Bible and mythology.

❺ ROTT CRYSTAL★

You can still read the name of the first owner on the neo-Renaissance facade of the most famous store in the city. Rott was also responsible for the construction of the Prague metro. This former hardware store was decorated by the painter Mikuláš Aleš and has been converted into a store selling high-quality crystalware on several floors.

Malé náměstí 3; ☎ 224 235 216
Every day Nov.-Mar. 10am-10pm (8pm Sun.); Apr.-Oct. 10am-8pm.

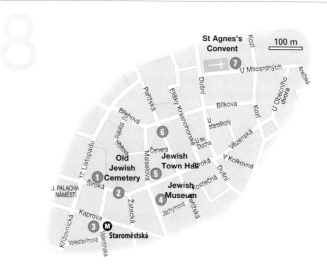

St Agnes's
Convent
Kozí
100 m
7
U Milosrdných
Anežská
Pařížská
Elišky Krásnohorské
Bílkova
Dušní
Kozí
U Obecního dvora
Obecní
Břehová
U starého Hřbitova
Červená
Maiselová
U sv. Ducha
U staréškoly
Vězeňská
Old Jewish Cemetery
1
Jewish Town Hall
6
5
Široká
V Kolkovně
17. Listopadu
J. PALACHA NÁMĚSTÍ
Široká
2
Žatecká
Jewish Museum
4
Kostečná
Dušní
Pařížská
Jáchymova
Kaprova
Křížovnická
Valentínska
Veleslavínova
3
M
Staroměstská

Josefov
and the Jewish ghetto

The Jewish quarter was named Josefov in recognition of Emperor Joseph II's alleviation of racial and religious discrimination against the Jews at the end of the 18th century. The ghetto deteriorated gradually and was almost reduced to rubble in 1893 by the city authorities, so that now only a few winding lanes remain. The Golem, Prague's notorious monster, is said to wander these streets at night.

scene. The oldest tomb dates back to 1439, the most recent one to 1787, and the most frequently visited one is that of Rabbi Löw (said to have given life to the monster Golem in the 16th century), in front of which people place stones and little notes containing prayers.

❶ Old Jewish Cemetery★★★

Široká 3
Opening hours: see Jewish Museum.

For three centuries, this narrow enclosure was the only authorized burial place for the Jewish community in Prague. Almost 100,000 people are said to be buried here and a tangle of 12,000 tombstones creates a staggeringly spectral

❸ Arzenal★

Valentinská 11
☎ 224 814 099
✆ 224 810 722
Every day 10am-midnight.

Designed by Bořek Šípek, who had been commissioned by Václav Havel to refurbish the castle, this elegant gallery with its colorful walls displays original and sometimes even extravagant creations by this famous designer. The delicious smells from the Thai

restaurant, also designed by Bořek Šipek, pervade the place.

❹ Jewish Museum★★

Tickets: U starého hřbitova 3 (☎ 222 317 191) and Maiselova 8-10 Nov.-Mar. Sun.-Fri. 9am-4.30pm; Apr.-Oct. 9am-6pm; closed during Jewish festivals. Information Center: U Stare Školy ☎ 224 819 456.

Only the Old-New Synagogue (see Don't Miss, p. 79) is still an active place of worship. The Maisel, Pinkas, Spanish and Klausen synagogues, as well as the Ceremonial Room, house the various sections of the Jewish Museum. Established in 1906, its collections increased in 1942 when the Nazis decided to keep confiscated items from the Jewish communities of Bohemia-Moravia here. The names of the 77,297 Czech victims of the genocide are written on the walls of the Pinkas synagogue, a memorial that is as sober as it is elegant. Drawings by children who had been deported to the Terezín camp are displayed on the first floor.

❺ Jewish Town Hall★

Maiselova 18 Closed to the public.

The seat of the Council of Jewish religious communities in the Czech Republic, this 16th-century building, capped with a green spire, was altered to the Rococo style in the 18th century.

❻ Pařížská★★

This vast avenue with its elegant neo-Baroque, neo-Gothic and Secession facades was based on Haussmann's Parisian model, hence its name. International airline offices and boutiques fill the ground floor premises. The road runs through the heart of Josefov.

❼ St Agnes's Convent★

U milosrdných 17 / Anezska 1 ☎ 224 81 06 28 Tue.-Sun. 10am-6pm (free on the first Wed. of the month 3-8pm).

Canonized on the eve of the Velvet Revolution, this convent was one of the main Bohemian religious centers. Restored during the 1960s, it now houses a museum dedicated to medieval art in Bohemia, Central Europe, Austria and Germany. Its rich collection of paintings and sculptures, remarkably displayed, is exceptional.

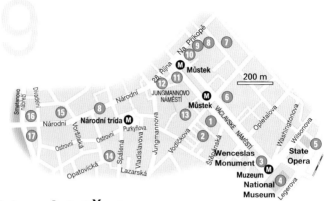

Nové Město,
the New Town

The New Town was founded in 1348 by Charles IV, after the Old Town had become too cramped. Nowadays, the "golden triangle," formed by Národní and Na příkopě streets with Wenceslas Square, is an important center for commerce, cafés and casinos. Once a horse market, it's now full of hotels, restaurants and stores. It's a hive of activity during the day, and at night the music from the clubs spills out onto the sidewalks. At all hours and in all weather, you'll see people strolling between stands on Wenceslas Square and tasting the sizzling *párek* (sausages served with sweet-and-sour mustard and chunks of bread).

❶ Václavské náměstí★★
(Wenceslas Square)

In its medieval days, Wenceslas Square was a horse market. Today it is a wide boulevard, partly pedestrianized, and Prague's own Champs-Elysées. It was here that independence was declared in 1918, that the Nazi occupation was challenged in 1938 and that

the huge spontaneous demonstrations took place before the Velvet Revolution in November 1989.

❸ Wenceslas Monument★

Near the equestrian statue of St Wenceslas, the focal point of the uprisings against the Communist regime in 1968 and 1989, is a small plaque commemorating the victims of Communism from 1948 to 1989. It also serves as a memorial to the student Jan Palach, who set himself on fire on January 16 1969, as a protest against the Russian occupation.

❹ National Museum★

Václavské nám. 68
☎ 224 497 111
Every day Oct.-Apr. 9am-5pm, May-Sep. 10am-6pm (closed the first Tue. of the month, free the first Mon. of the month)
Entrance charge.

This museum was completed in 1890 and dominates Wenceslas Square as a rather pompous statement of nationalism. Its dusty natural history collections contrast awkwardly with the kitsch splendor of its pantheon, containing statues of Czech scholars, writers and artists.

⑤ State Opera★

Státní Opera

Wilsonova 4
☎ 224 227 266
www.opera.cz

This building opened in 1888 as the New German Theater and was intended to be a rival to the magnificent Czech National Theater (see p. 63), which had an exclusively Czech repertoire. It is a smaller replica of the Vienna Opera, but the adjacent freeway sadly spoils its neo-Classical facade.

⑥ Europa Hotel café★★★

Václavské nám. 25
☎ 224 22 81 17
Every day 10am-10pm.

An art-nouveau masterpiece, this café was completed in 1904 and is a compulsory stop on your itinerary. Its interior is rather shabby due to lack of repair, but the café has a wonderful Middle European charm and a colorful clientele. It's a reminder of the golden age of hotels, with its original bars, mirrors and wood paneling.

⑦ Mucha Museum

Panská 7
☎ 224 215 409
Every day 10am-6pm
See Don't Miss, p. 70.

Located in a charming Baroque palace, this museum is dedicated to the famous Czech herald of art nouveau who produced, among other things, beautiful posters for Sarah Bernhardt. The exhibition, concentrating mainly on his time in Paris (the best-known period), contains around 100 works of art: oil paintings, drawings, pastels, posters, decorative panels and photographs.

❷ LUCERNA★

In the 1920s, Václav Havel's grandfather designed Prague's most famous arcade in Moorish style. The Lucerna Palace is enormous and houses cafés, restaurants, shops, a movie theater, a nightclub and a ballroom. The traditional graduation dances are held here (see p. 27), and a famous jazz festival, held since 1964, takes place in October, attracting international musicians. Gilbert Bécaud, a popular French singer, drew a crowd of 3,000 local fans here in the 1960s. An extremely popular concert venue.

Access via Štěpánská 61 or Vodičkova 36.

❽ Národní třída and Na příkopě ★
(National Avenue and Moat Avenue)

These two avenues followed the course of the Old Town moat until 1760, and they still mark the border between the Old and New Towns. Partly pedestrianized, they became the main promenades for the Czech and German bourgeoisie at the turn of the century. The boulevards are full of stores and restaurants, banks and clubs, but don't forget to take a look at Národní třída, 40. The "rondo-cubist" architecture of the Adria Palace (1922–25) will take you by surprise. It was here that the first of Václav Havel's meetings of the civic forum took place in 1989.

❾ Muzeum Komunismu
Na příkopě 10
☎ 224 212 966
Every day 9am-9pm.

Located on the main shopping street in town, this museum relates the history of Czech communism, from the creation of Czechoslovakia in 1918 until the Velvet Revolution in 1989. Various media, among which are many photographs, enable the visitor to relive the main events, sometimes tragic ones, which punctuated that era. Explanatory texts are also in English.

❿ Koruna Palac
Václavské náměstí 1
☎ 224 219 526
Mon.-Sat. 9am-8pm,
Sun. 10am-8pm.

At the corner of Na příkopě and Wencelas Square, this art-nouveau apartment building,

built in 1912, is topped with a beautiful octagonal dome (*koruna*), typical of this colorful geometric style. The building, which has been carefully restored, has retained its beautiful reliefs, windows and stained glass embellished with gold. Today it houses a modern shopping arcade comprising some 25 boutiques and a café-restaurant.

⓫ Bat'a Store ★
Václavské nám. 6
☎ 224 21 81 33
Mon.-Fri. 9am-9pm, Sat. 9am-8pm, Sun. 10am-8pm.

This famous Czech shoe brand name was established in 1894 and was finally restored in 1992 to its former owners, who had been in exile in Canada. The shoes remain the same as

ever, but the functional style of architecture is certainly worth a look. Tomáš Bat'a, to whom the company was restored, began his working life here as a salesman in the 1930s, and you may run into his heirs to the empire.

⓬ U Pinkasu
Jungmannova namesti 16
☎ 221 111 150
Every day 8am-2am.

This former traditional *hospoda*, entirely rebuilt in 2002 and mainly patronized by locals, is the ideal place to enjoy a cool *Plzensky Prazdoj* beer or savor delicious traditional Czech dishes. The *gulas* and the *svíčková* (beef filet with herbs) served with *knedliky* dumplings are particularly tasty.

⓭ Franciscan Garden★

Jungmannovo nám. 18
Every day 6am-7pm.

Just next to the Gothic St Mary-of-the-Snows Church (Panna Maria Sněžká) is a haven of greenery and tranquility. Originally the healing garden of a Franciscan monastery, elderly ladies come here to chat over an ice cream, and local workers eat their lunch on the white wooden benches. The garden has been

open to the public since 1950. Escape the bustle of Wenceslas Square and enjoy this oasis.

⓮ Velryba★

(The Whale)
Opatovická 24
☎ 224 931 444
Every day 11am-midnight.

If, like Jonah, you wander into "The Whale," you'll have

discovered one of the best cafés in Prague. It's one of the increasingly popular "gallery-cafés." Literary and artistic locals come to read their papers on splendid mahogany tables and to enjoy good food at reasonable prices, including a selection of vegetarian dishes. Those in the know go straight to the back room, which is more comfortable with its welcoming chairs.

⓯ Praha and Topič buildings★

Národní 7 and 9.

Osvald Polivka designed two buildings in the art nouveau style. It's interesting to compare Praha and its stunning mosaics inspired by the Viennese Secession, with Topič, whose much more ostentatious facade was influenced by the German Jugendstil. Praha was built for the Prague insurance company of the same name. A modest employee by the name of Franz Kafka worked there for several years (see p. 16).

⓰ Café Slavia★★

Národní 1
☎ 224 218 493
Every day 8am-11pm.

This is one of the most mythical cafés in Central Europe, with huge picture windows and panoramic views

of the Castle. It was closed in 1992, an event which gave rise to many indignant petitions. Six years later it opened its doors again, having been tastefully renovated. It is the old friend of dissidents and artists, and once more the favorite haunt of Prague's intelligentsia. They serve a strong but quite legal absinthe, whose inebriating powers need to be treated with the greatest respect.

⓱ National Theater★★

(Národní divadlo)
Národní 2
☎ 224 901 111.

This theater is a proud symbol of the Czech national identity. It was financed entirely by private subscriptions but was destroyed by fire the year it was opened. A second patriotic donation of money made possible the reconstruction of this impressive neo-Renaissance building on the edge of the Vltava river. Completed in just two years, it is a powerful symbol in a country whose first elected president post Communism was a man of the theater himself. The theater was restored during the late 1970s when Karel Prager built the New Stage.

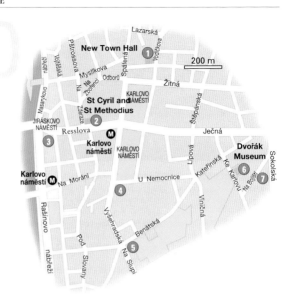

Karlovo náměstí

It was once the cattle market when Charles IV founded the New Town in 1348, but it is now the main commercial district. Those living near the river walk their dogs in Charles Square, trams cross its main streets and everything seems calm and peaceful. However, do not be deceived. It was here that Faust dabbled in black magic and made a pact with the devil.

❶ New Town Hall★

Karlovo nám. 23
☎ 224 947 131
Tower: Tue.-Sun. 10am-6pm May-Sep.; exhibition halls: Tue.-Sun. 10am-5.30pm.

On the largest square in Prague stands this fine Gothic hall, which houses prestigious exhibitions and can be rented for lavish wedding receptions. It was here that the first "defenestration" in Prague took place. During a Hussite revolt on July 30, 1419, the burghers were thrown out of the windows and landed on the pikes of the Hussites. A statue of Hussite preacher Jan Želivsjký commemorates this.

❷ Church of St Cyril and St Methodius★

Resslova 9
Mon.-Sat. 9-11am.

This Baroque church, built in the 1730s, became the base for the Czechoslovak Orthodox Church in 1935 and was

rededicated to the two saints. These brothers, known as "Apostles to the Slavs" brought Christianity to Moravia in the 9th century. In 1942, the parachutists who had assassinated the Nazi governor of Czechoslovakia, Reinhard Heydrich, hid in the church, and you can still see the bullet holes left in the crypt by the machine guns used against them. They took their own lives rather than surrender.

❸ Ginger and Fred★★

Rašínovo nábř. 80
☎ 221 98 41 60
Mon. 7pm-10.30pm; Tue.-Sat. noon-2pm and 7-10.30pm.

The Canadian-born Frank Gehry and the Yugoslav-born Vlado Milunic designed this glass building. It looks rather like a couple dancing, hence its nickname. The fashionable

French restaurant, *La Perle de Prague*, is housed here. Before moving to a more discreet home, Václav Havel lived next door.

❺ The Botanical Garden★

Na Slupi 18
☎ 224 918 970
Garden: every day 10am-6pm
Greenhouses (entrance fee): every day 10am-4pm.

Laid out at the end of the 19th century, this small garden belonging to the university is a peaceful haven where you can relax, only two minutes' walk from Karlovo Square (tram no.18). Its charming paths edged with flower borders and colorful shrubs whose names are clearly labeled meander pleasantly around beautiful large greenhouses built in 1938.

❻ Dvořák Museum★★

Ke Karlovu 20
☎ 224 923 363
Tue.-Sun. 10am-5pm.

The Dvořák Museum not only houses the composer's piano, desk and viola, but also has some more unusual memorabilia, such as a handkerchief, cuffs, a hat and a medicine case. This beautiful Baroque villa, dating from the 18th century is hidden at the

bottom of a garden. Formerly the second home of a rich Bohemian family, it became known as Villa Amerika after a nearby inn. It was a perfect name for the composer of the *New World Symphony*.

❼ U Kalicha★

Na Bojišti 12-14
☎ 224 912 557
Every day 11am-11pm.

The atmosphere in this pub has much in common with a Munich *Oktoberfest* with beer served in large jugs. It is based on the theme of the famous Czech comic character, the good soldier Švejk. Jaroslav Hašek's hero walks in and suddenly finds himself arrested in connection with the assassination of Archduke Ferdinand. Traditional Czech cuisine is served, but it tends to be tourists rather than locals who come to eat here.

❹ FAUST HOUSE★

A mysterious aura surrounds this Baroque house, where it is claimed that the devil abducted Faust. The English adventurer and alchemist, Edward Kelley, came to live here but was later thrown in prison by Emperor Rudolph II. He failed to reveal the secret of the philosopher's stone to the emperor, a great believer in necromancy. Appropriately enough, there is now a pharmacy on the first floor of the building.

Karlovo nám. 40-41
Closed to the public.

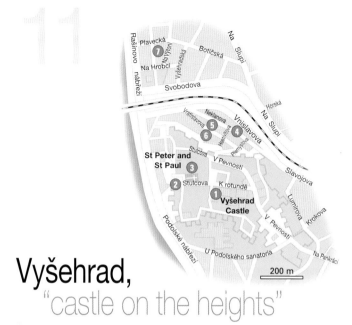

Vyšehrad,
"castle on the heights"

Vyšehrad, standing above the Vltava river, holds a very special place in the hearts of the Czech people. It has great mythological and historical importance, and according to Czech legend, it's the place where the Slav tribes first settled in Prague. Join the locals, who come here for a quiet family stroll. It's a perfect spot to escape the crowds and see Prague Castle from another viewpoint. Don't miss the opportunity to see the cubist villas.

❶ Vyšehrad Castle★★

Access via U Pevnosti 5
☎ **241 410 352**
Every day Apr.-Oct. 9.30am-6pm, Nov.-Mar. 9.30am-5pm.

Vratislav II, first king of Bohemia, founded the castle in the 11th century, but it was later superseded by Prague Castle, which was easier to defend. Abandoned after its destruction during the Hussite wars, it was then transformed into a powerful fortress in the 17th century. The restored St Martin's rotunda is the sole survivor of the medieval fortress. Vyšehrad is now a symbol of Czech nationhood.

❷ Church of St Peter and St Paul★★

Same as Vyšehrad Castle.
Josef Mocker built this neo-Gothic church in 1885 on the foundations of the 11th-century basilica, commissioned by Vratislav II. In the adjoining garden there are four statues of legendary figures from Czech mythology by Josef Myslbek.

❸ Vyšehrad Cemetery★★

Same as Vyšehrad Castle.
See Don't Miss, p. 78.

As the name suggests, the interior of this beer hall has a marine theme. Fish nets hang in the windows and the bar is shaped like a ship's prow. Excellent beer is served, but do remember that you're in a landlocked country when choosing your meal. Avoid the frozen fish dishes and opt instead for the rustic Czech specialties, such as *bramborák*, which is a delicious potato pancake.

As a tribute to the role they played in the foundation of the nation, the grateful citizens gave this cemetery over to the key artists and intellectuals involved. Buried here are the authors Jan Neruda, Vítězslav Nezval and Karel Čapek (famous as the inventor of the word "robot"), together with the composers Bedřich Smetana and Antonín Dvořák, whose memorial is very elaborate with a mosaic inscription. The painter Alphonse Mucha also

lies in the cemetery, which was founded in 1869.

❹ Czech cubism★★★

The villas in Vyšehrad were all built between 1911 and 1913 in the cubist style that was very popular in Prague at the time.

Take a tour of the buildings, beginning at Neklanova, 30, with Josef Chochol's impressive structure. Notice the door handles but avoid the restaurant inside. Further along at no. 2, you'll be able to admire Antonín Belada's cubist facade. Finish off your walk with a visit to two more of Chochol's works. At Libušina, 49, look at his cleverly designed triangular garden, and at Rašínovo ná břeží, 6, 8 and 10 cast your eye over the elegant house he designed, which is large enough for three families.

❺ U zlaté kotvy★

(The Golden Anchor)
Vratislavova 19
☎ 224 910 438
Every day 10am-midnight.

❼ THE LEGEND OF PRINCESS LIBUŠE

Princess Libuše is said to have prophesied the future glory of Prague from the top of Vyšehrad. From 710 she ruled over a people reluctant to be led by a woman. They soon demanded that she took a husband. Libuše chose a man called Přemysl (meaning plowman) and founded the Přemyslid dynasty, which ruled over Bohemia until the 14th century.

❻ Daič ceramics workshop★★

Vratislavova 38, Prague 2
☎ 737 803 261
Mon.-Sat. 10am-6pm.

Devoted to pottery, the Daič family reveres Czech clay, particularly from the region of Hradec Králové. They have been working with it for the past 12 years. As you push open the door of the family workshop, you'll discover Patrik behind his potter's wheel and his wife, Andrea, at the kiln. They will immediately stop what they are doing to show you (with a smile) what they produce: cups, saucers, vases, containers, water jugs embellished with enameled country landscapes.

Museum of Modern
and Contemporary Art

The Museum of Modern and Contemporary Art has a fine collection of 19th- and 20th-century European art. The palace was originally built to house international fairs. Among other features of its extraordinary architecture, the building's four stories are built around a central well of light.

The building
Built in 1929, the Palace of International Fairs changed hands in 1995. Don't miss the impressive view, from the first floor, of the balconies hanging in midair. The bookstore contains many interesting publications on Czech art.

Third floor
The projection room near the entrance shows animated films from the 1930s. The puppets of Trnka (1912–62), one of the first animated film

directors, are exhibited in window displays. After viewing Toyen's surrealist paintings, don't miss the photographs by Rössler (1902–90) and Funke (1896–1945). A space is dedicated to social realism, the official art of the cold war period.

Fourth floor
Dedicated to 19th- and 20th-century French art, this floor contains two remarkable self-portraits by Picasso (1907) and Douanier Rousseau (1890, the only one he ever did).

Fourth floor
From the poetic realism of the *Union of souls* (1896) by Švabinský (1873–1962), to the exquisite portrait of the *Lady with the Camellia* (1850) by Mánes (1793–1858) and the humorous depiction of Czech society by Navrátil (1798–1855), they all bear witness to the intensity of artistic exchanges between Paris and Prague. On your way out, don't miss the sculptor B. Kafka's (1878–1942) melancholy *Broken Life*.

INFORMATION
Národní Veletržní palác
Dukelských hrdnů 47
☎ 224 30 11 11
Tue.-Sun. 10am-6pm
Entrance charge.

Museum of
Decorative Arts

Meissen porcelain, as well as art-nouveau pieces such as the famous ashtrays and sugar bowls of Janák and Hofman.

The museum exhibits a wide variety of works from its collection of Bohemian and Central European decorative arts from the 16th to 19th centuries. The museum is slightly run down and would greatly benefit from a general overhaul, but its extraordinary contents and atmosphere are full of charming surprises.

Furniture
Fine examples of sculpted furniture from the time of Rudolph II, rare pieces from the Renaissance, and cubist creations by Janák.

Books and posters
In the area dedicated to the history of printing, you'll find a Czech Bible from 1506, and a collection of posters spanning the period between 1850 and 1935.

Photography
A small collection containing remarkable works from the 1920s and 1930s by Drtikol and Sudek.

Glassworks
The art of Bohemian glass was born in the Middle Ages, but started to thrive with the arrival of the famous engraver Lehman at the court of Rudolph II. Next to the collections from the 16th to 19th centuries, a display maps the evolution of glassware from antiquity to art nouveau, through the Middle Ages, the Renaissance, Baroque and Rococo.

Fabrics
A fine display of 19th century women's costumes, 17th-century silk cloths, fine lace from the 19th century and modern creations such as Paličková's (1926), whose style is reminiscent of Léger.

Ceramics and porcelain
A beautiful collection of ceramics and 18th-century

INFORMATION

Umĕleckoprůmyslové (Decorative Arts) Museum (see p. 51)
17. Listopadu 2
☎ 251 093 296
Tue.-Sun. 10am-6pm.

Mucha Museum

Since 1997, the Kaunický has been the home of the Mucha Museum and its drawings, lithographs and personal effects. An opportunity to rediscover the art-nouveau movement, of which Czech artist Alphonse Mucha (1860–1936) became one of the most gifted masters.

Mucha and Paris

At the age of 19, having been turned down by the Prague Art Academy, Mucha left his Moravian home to settle in Vienna. However, it was in Paris that he achieved inter-national fame. On Christmas eve of 1894, Mucha met Sarah Bernhardt, and started to work on a poster for her performance of *Gismonda* (see the originals in Section 2), the start of a long and fruitful collaboration. Photographs show his Parisian studio, a meeting place for Parisian artists and intellectuals.

Decorative arts

Convinced that the artist's role was to embellish and enhance everyday life, Mucha had the idea of creating decorative panels, full of his famous floral motifs and arabesques, and producing them in unlimited series. In 1902, he published an encyclopedia of decorative arts for the benefit of craftsmen, adapting his personal style to the work of metal, glass and leather.

The Slavic soul

In 1910, Mucha returned to his homeland, devoting himself to the *Slav Epic*, the Town Hall and the Municipal House, while at the same time creating posters for theater performances, postage stamps and paper money! The exhibition ends with *France kissing Bohemia* (1918).

INFORMATION

Mucha Museum
(see p. 61)
Kaunický Palace
Panská 7, Prague 1
☎ 224 216 415
museum@mucha.cz
http://www.mucha.cz
Every day 10am–6pm
Entrance charge.

Municipal House

This masterpiece of art nouveau celebrated its 90th anniversary in 2002. Reception halls, exhibition spaces, a coffee shop, two restaurants and one of Prague's largest concert halls (1,500 seats) make it one of the city's main cultural attractions.

having given full rein to his inspiration. From the sinuous floral motifs of German Jungendstil (1894–1914) to the sober geometrical lines of the Viennese Secession (1897–1907), it is the cross-fertilization of these architectural currents which gave birth to the exuberance of Prague's own variety of art nouveau. The facade was built in the neo-Baroque style while the interiors are all art nouveau.

The former Royal Palace

The Municipal House was erected on the site of the former Royal Palace, the residence of kings from 1383 to 1485. Swept away by the modernist fever of the early 20th century, it was pulled down in 1903 to make way for the Municipal House. Inaugurated in 1912, it was equipped with state-of-the-art central heating, air-conditioning, drinking water and mechanical elevators.

The style

The Municipal House is a patchwork of different architectural styles, each artist

The decoration

The municipality called on Prague's most prestigious artists to work on the interior decoration. Aleš, Mucha, Preisler, Wenig and Švabinský contributed paintings, frescoes and stained-glass windows, while Mařatka, Myslbek, Šaloun and B. Kafka produced the sculptures.

Highlights

The mosaic above the entrance's metal marquee is Špillar's homage to Prague's revolutionary spirit. In the mayor's office, you will find Mucha's allegorical paintings dedicated to the civic virtues.

In the Smetana concert hall, on each side of the stage, are two sculpted groups by Šaloun, symbolizing Smetana's *Ma vlast* and Dvořák's *Slavic dances*. In the small reception rooms on the second floor, the frescoes are by Švabinský. Finally, no tour of the Municipal House would be complete without a visit of the basement inn, the magnificent French restaurant on the first floor and the coffee shop.

INFORMATION

Municipal House
(see p. 55)
Obecní dům
Náměstí Republiky 5,
Prague 1
☎ 222 002 101
info@obecni-dum
www.obecni-dum.cz
Every day 10am-6pm.
Opening hours on
the website
Guided tours only.

Church of Our Lady before Týn

It's gigantic spires stand in the heart of the old city. Originally a modest Romanesque church frequented by local tradesmen, it became a Gothic cathedral in the 13th century and was rebaptized Our Lady before Týn a century later. It was Prague's main Hussite church.

Highlights

The three naves and choirs are the work of Parleř's studio, the chief architect of Charles IV. A fire destroyed the central nave in 1689, which was subsequently rebuilt in the Gothic style. On the fourth pillar to the left, the magnificent stone Gothic baldachin was built by Rejsek in 1493. Prague's oldest surviving baptistery (1414) is located in the lateral choir of the south nave. On the altar stands a magnificent Gothic calvary from the 15th century.

Paintings

The painting on the master altar representing the Assumption of the Virgin and the Holy Trinity, as well as the painting hanging from the columns on both sides, were executed between 1648 and 1660 by Škréta, Bohemia's first Baroque painter. To the right of the central nave of the church, next to the fifth pillar, is the tomb of Tycho Brahé (1546–1601), Danish astrologer to the court of Rudolph II.

Anecdote

At the time when Franz Kafka's family occupied the adjacent "Three Kings" house (602 Celetná Street), he was in the habit of looking inside the church from a small window which opened on the building's south wall, fascinated by its mysterious atmosphere.

INFORMATION

Church of Our Lady before Týn
(see p. 57)
Chrám matky boží před týnem
Staroměstské nám. 14, entrance via number 604 in the Old Town Place.
Mon.-Fri. 9am-noon and 1-2pm.
Services: Sat. 8am, Sun. 9.30am and 9pm.

St Vitus Cathedral

Part of the Castle, this is Bohemia's largest religious sanctuary: 125m (410ft) long, 60m (197ft) wide and 33m (108ft) high. Building began in 1344, under the direction of Mathieu d'Arras, a master of the Gothic style, and was continued by Parléř. Consecrated in 1385, it was only completed in 1929!

Mucha's stained-glass window

In the archbishops' new chapel, on the left, after the entrance, don't miss Mucha's magnificent stained-glass window representing St Cyril and St Methodius (1931). The artist's grandson is portrayed at the feet of St Wenceslas.

The golden gate

Under the reign of Chales IV, the main entrance was the golden gate on the southern facade. It owes its name to the red and gold mosaic (1371) representing Judgment Day and featuring Charles IV and his wife.

The tomb of St John Nepocumeme

Because he had refused to betray the secret of the queen's confession, Wenceslas IV had him thrown off Charles Bridge in 1393. He was canonized in 1729. His tomb (1733–36) was designed by Fischer von Erlach, and required two tons of silver.

The St Wenceslas Chapel (1362–67)

Built by Parléř over Wenceslas' grave, the chapel's fresco is composed of 1345 semi-precious stones which were set using a gold-based mortar. The lower paintings (1367) represent the passion and those above the life of St Wenceslas (1507–09).

The treasure room

Protected by seven locks, the treasure room is home to Bohemia's crown jewels. Local legend has it that Wenceslas hung himself from the door knob.

INFORMATION

St Vitus Cathedral
Chrám Svatého Víta
(see p. 36)
Third courtyard of the Castle.
Entrance via the three porches
(east side)
Every day: Apr.-Sep. 9am-5pm, Oct.-Mar.: 9am-4pm.

Church of St Nicholas
of Malá Strana

In 1625 the Jesuits, whom Ferdinand II of Hapsburg had asked to convert Bohemia to Catholicism, were allocated a Gothic church founded in 1283. In 1653, Italian architects started to work on its restoration, creating the jewel of Prague Baroque, and the masterpiece of the Dientzenhofers.

Dientzenhofer

In 1704, the Dientzenhofer family, the masters of Bohemian high Baroque, started working on the church. Kristof gave us the facade and the nave, his son Kilián Ignác, the choir and the cupola (1722) and his stepson Lugaro, the bell tower and the interiors (1751–56).

Interior

On the ceiling, Kracher produced the largest painting of 18th-century Prague (1,500sq m/16,000sq ft), celebrating the apotheosis of St Nicholas. Above the great organ, the *Apotheosis of St Cecilia*, the patron saint of musicians, is by Palko. In the central nave, the *Glorification of the life of St Nicholas* is by Kracher. In the cupola above the choir, you can admire a fresco 30m (230ft) in diameter by Palko, the *Glory of the Holy Trinity* (1752–53). The four neo-Classical sculptures of the Church Fathers are by Platzer (1768–69). The pulpit's delicate motifs and angels are by Prachner (1765). In the lateral chapels, you will notice the sculptures by Platzer and the fresco by Hager, Kracher and Kramolin.

Concerts

In 1787, Mozart performed on the organ, with its 2,500 pipes. Three days after his untimely death in 1791, a requiem drew a crowd of 4,000. The acoustics are exceptional, and concerts are still performed here.

INFORMATION

Church of St Nicholas of Malá Strana
(see p. 46)
Kostel sv. Mikuláše
Malostranské náměstí
☎ 257 534 215
Every day 9am–5pm
Entrance charge
Information about concerts at entrance.

Stahov Convent
Library

Founded in 1143 by Vladislav II, the monastery is the most ancient convent of the Premonstratensians, as well as Bohemia's largest Romanesque monument. It was rebuilt several times, and completed in the Baroque era. The convent owes its fame to its library and the magnificent rooms dedicated to Philosophy and Theology.

The Theology Room

The abbot's library, called the Theological Room, contains 16,000 books, mostly Bibles. The 17 brightly colored frescoes were painted between 1723 and 1727 by the monk Nosecký. They represent Wisdom being derived from the rational study of God.

The Philosophy Room

The Philosophy Room contains 50,000 books of philosophy, history and philology. The Baroque shelves come from the Premonstratensian monastery of Louka. The superb Baroque fresco on the ceiling is the last work of Viennese painter Maulbertsch. In an allegory of Wisdom and Human Progress, inspired by the optimism of the Enlightenment, one can recognize Moses and the Ten Commandments and St Paul preaching at the altar.

The collection

In 1950, the library contained 130,000 books, 2,000 of which date back to the 15th century, and 3,000 manuscripts. Nowadays, with the addition of the Literature Museum collection, it contains 980,000

books, the oldest of which is the Strahov Gospel, illuminated in the 9th and 10th centuries, in the reign of Charles IV, and a 1476 printed Czech gospel.

INFORMATION

Strahov Monastery
(see p. 41)
Klášter premonstrátů na
Strahově
Strahovské nádvoří 1
☎ 220 516 654
Every day 9am-noon, 1-5pm
Entrance charge.

Charles Bridge

It's impossible to avoid Charles Bridge. Always extremely busy, whatever the season, it's better to wait for nightfall to cross the Vltava under the dim glow of the street lamps, surrounded by statues, while admiring the panorama of the Castle and giving in to the place's irresistible charm.

Construction

In 1357, Charles IV laid the foundation stone of the Charles Bridge on the ruins of the Judith Bridge. The bridge, 1,520m (5,000ft) long, 9m (30ft) wide and resting on 16 pillars, was completed in 1402, becoming a central witness to Prague's history, with its coronations and royal funerals, its jousts and tournaments, and the tragic beheadings of 1621.

The towers

The small Malá Strana tower belonged to the Judith Bridge. The larger one was built in 1464. The scars visible under the Gothic arch were caused by crossbows. The Old Town Tower, a Gothic masterpiece and one of the 15th century's most beautiful doors, was damaged by Swedish artillery in 1648. Between Charles IV and Wenceslas stands St Vitus, the bridge's protector.

The sculptures

The Baroque statues of Braun and Brokof were added to the bridge's wooden cross in the 17th century. The first statue was one of *St John Nepomucene* by Brokof (1683). Touching the saint is said to bring good luck. The bridge's most beautiful Baroque masterpiece is *St Luitgarde* (1710) which Braun sculpted when he was 26. Under the *Pietà* (1859), a cage was used to lower dishonest merchants into the water.

INFORMATION

Karlův Most
(see p. 50)
Charles Bridge connects the Old City to Malá Strana from Křížovnické Place to Mostecká.

Nerudova Street

In order to reach the castle using the royal route, you must walk up Nerudova Street. The road is lined with remarkable bourgeois houses and Baroque palaces, splendidly decorated and displaying the painted street signs typical of Prague. If you look carefully, you might even see remains of Renaissance architecture.

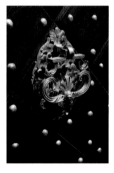

Kolovrat Palace, built between 1721 and 1726 over an earlier Renaissance palace. The portal is guarded by two magnificent eagles by Braun. At no. 33, the small balcony of the old Bretfeld Palace (1765) witnessed the arrival of Mozart, Casanova and the entire Prague aristocracy.

Jan Neruda

The street owes its name to the poet Jan Neruda (1834–91), who was born here and wrote the *Tales of Malá Strana*. Between 1845 and 1857, he lived at "The Two suns," at no. 47, with its remarkable Baroque facade (1673–90), and later moved to no. 44, the "Three black eagles."

Street signs

In the Middle Ages, these banners were posted to identify the houses, their owners and their profession. Numbers appeared in 1770.

Beautiful facades

At no. 2, U Kocoura has a half-Baroque, half-neo-Classical facade and a Renaissance portal. At no. 5, the Morzin Palace is occupied by the Romanian embassy. In 1713–14, Santini remodeled the building by connecting four separate houses. On the main entrance portal, which is slightly off-center, are two sculptures by Brokoff, whose signature is still visible, representing day (on the left) and night (on the right). Two gigantic Moors support the balcony. You will notice the coat of arms of Count Morzin who fought against the Moors. No. 12, "The three violins," was the home to three generations of string instrument makers. The Italian embassy at no. 20 occupies the Thun-Hohenstein-

INFORMATION

Nerudova Street runs from Malostranské Place (at the foot of the Castle) to Hradčanské náměstí. (see p. 46).

Vyšehrad Cemetery

If you go to Vyšehrad, you should visit its cemetery. Every year, coinciding with the start of the Prague Spring International Music Festival, a Mass is celebrated at the grave of Smetana, on May 12, the anniversary of his death, followed by a performance of *Ma Vlast* at the Municipal House.

History

In 1875, in the heat of the country's national revolution, the intelligentsia turned to Vyšehrad to honor the nation's great men. In an area stepped in myth and legend, the cemetery became the resting place for 600 important people. The tombstones were all created by great artists of the time, a tradition which has survived until the present day.

The celebrities

The first man to be buried here was Hanka, famous for having forged manuscripts which he claimed were the first to have been written in Czech (no. 277). The tomb of the writer Čapek at no. 107 was conceived by his brother in honor of the Czechoslovak Republic. Under the neo-Renaissance arches at no. 20 lie the composer Dvořák and his wife.

In the eastern part of the cemetery, a small pantheon called the Slavin contains the tombs of some 50 important people. Among them are Mucha, Myslbek and the poet Zeyer, author of the Vyšehrad poem, which Smetana used for his *Ma Vlast* symphony. The great composer's tomb is at no. 329, next to the pantheon. To the south, near to the entrance, lie the tombs of the Elizabethan nuns.

INFORMATION

Vyšehradský hřbitov
(see p. 66)
Every day 8am-7pm
(Nov.-Feb. 9am-4pm,
Mar.-Apr. 8am-6pm)
Free entrance.
Numbers in the text refer to the numbered graves shown at the entrance of the cemetery.

The Old-New Synagogue

Built at the end of the 13th century, the oldest synagogue in Prague is also the oldest building in the ghetto, razed and rebuilt at the beginning of the 20th century. A place of worship for over 700 years, a refuge for the Jewish community during the dark periods over the centuries, it remains at the center of the religious life of the Jews of Prague.

Between legend and reality

It is said that when this synagogue was first built, several white stone walls were uncovered and identified as those of a synagogue thanks to the discovery of a scroll from the *Torah* and prayer books in Hebrew. It was then decided to build the synagogue with these stones and to call it the Old-New. Another version of the story tells how it was first called the "New" Synagogue, but renamed "Old-New" in the 16th century, when other places of worship were built.

A stark style

This building in the primitive Gothic style remains the last example of a medieval synagogue in Europe. Adorned with a brick gable, its austere front hides a very stark interior reached via a rather narrow staircase, open on the south side. In the entrance hall, the door to the prayer room is embellished with a beautiful sculpted tympanum.

The prayer room

A narrow double nave, split into two-by-two octagonal pillars, is capped by a five-ribbed vault. The capitals of the columns are decorated with vine leaves, a symbol of fertility. In the center, the pulpit is encircled with a wrought-iron grid in the flamboyant Gothic style. In the walls, small grooved windows look onto the women's gallery which was added in the 18th century.

INFORMATION

Old-New Synagogue
(see p. 59)
Staronova synagoga
Červená 2
Apr.-Oct. Fri. 9am-5pm,
Sun.-Thu. 9am-6pm;
Nov.-Mar. Fri. 9am-2pm,
Sun.-Thu. 9am-4.30pm
Entrance charge.

Practicalities

Hotels in Prague are generally expensive. The renovated hotels are both smart and pricey, whereas good budget accommodations are more difficult to find. If you are looking for food, you'll find excellent restaurants in the city center. You can also choose a typical inn to sample a Czech specialty such as a juicy duck washed down with beer.

Hotels

There's not much to be found in Prague between the four-star hotel and the small pension. Accommodations are expensive in the historic center (Prague 1), given the average Czech salary (about US$700 in 2005). In the suburbs and the other districts prices fall dramatically, but so does the romantic setting!

Classification

Hotels are listed according to the number of stars, from one to five. These are supposed to correspond to criteria of comfort, location and price.

Five-star hotels offer double bedrooms for approximately Kč4,500–8,500 per night. In the city center, you'll find it difficult to find a double bedroom with bathroom for less than Kč3,000. For young people, there are cheap hotels offered in the summer in apartment blocks. Contact www.travellers.cz and www.applehostels.cz.

Hotel reservations

Demand for hotel rooms exceeds supply in Prague. If your travel package does not include a room, it is advisable to make a reservation by telephone or on the Internet in advance, even in the less busy periods. During Easter, between July and August and at New Year, you should reserve your accommodations ahead.

Restaurants

In the historic parts of Prague 1 the inexpensive inns of the past have now been replaced by gastronomic restaurants, often inspired by French or Italian cuisine. Prices have escalated with the advent of three-course menus (appetizer, main course,

LAST-MINUTE ACCOMMODATIONS

PragueCheapFlats

No point looking any further: you will not come across a better reservation agency for finding cheap and well-located accommodations in Prague. All you need to do is send a reservation form by email with an outline of what you're looking for. You can expect an answer within 48 hours. You will then be put in contact with the owners of the flat, whom you will pay directly, in Czech crowns.

info@praguecheapflats.com; www.praguecheapflats.com

E-travel.cz

This online agency (in English) offers, among other services, a wide choice of hotel rooms and apartments at very attractive prices.

Ostrovní 7, Prague 1; ☎ 224 990 990; ✆ 224 990 999 www.travel.cz

dessert). Allow around Kč1,500 not including wine. You may prefer to opt for a *hospoda* (brasserie) where you'll be served typical Czech cuisine. Here you'll be able to enjoy a single, often plentiful, dish (for example crispy duck) with a beer. Allow around Kč250. The Czechs have dinner fairly early (around 7pm) and then meet up in bar to have the obligatory beer, or to go to the opera.

Czech etiquette

If you choose a typical Czech inn, you may find yourself joining others at a table, but there is no obligation to enter into a conversation with your neighbors. It is customary to have your plate taken away as soon as you've finished your meal, even if your fellow diners are still in the middle of eating. A glass of soda water (*soda*) or mineral water (*mineralka*) will sometimes be brought to the table. In some establishments your beer will be replaced automatically once your glass is empty. Don't hesitate to refuse, even

if there is some pressure to continue drinking.

The check

When the check arrives, examine it carefully. You may find that an extra cover charge

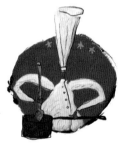

or a charge for the bread has been added. A main meal won't usually include vegetables or rice. When you're ready to pay, add a tip of 5 to 10 percent to the check. Let the waiter know and it will be deducted as a tip from your change. Don't leave the money on the table.

Vegetarian dishes

Restaurant menus do feature dishes without meat (*jídla bez*

masa), However, this does not necessarily mean that they are lighter. You could try the dumplings with scrambled egg (*knedlíky vejci*), the breaded and fried cheese (*smažený sýr*) or mushrooms (*smažené žampióny*). It is also worth sampling the tofu dishes (*sojové maso*).

Places to eat

Samoobsluha: These are self-service snack bars with minimal seating, where you can get great-value hot meals. They're usually non-smoking.

Pivnice, hospoda, hostinec: These are all pubs, where you'll find that most Czechs go to eat and drink.

Vinarna: You may be able to get a snack in these popular wine bars.

Restaurace: This is the equivalent of a restaurant, though the menu here may differ little from that of a *hospoda*.

Cukrarna: Try the delicious pastries at these cafés – they're great value! A croissant (*loupák*) will cost about Kč12. The traditional pastry is known as *koláč* and is served with plum jam (*povidlový*) or poppy seed jam (*makový*).

FINDING YOUR WAY

We have divided hotels, restaurants and other attractions into districts to make it easier to find somewhere local to the area you have chosen to visit. You will often find more detailed directions on the websites of the individual places listed.

Hotels

1 - U Karlova Mostu
2 - Hotel Neruda
3 - Hotel Kampa
4 - U Páva

Malá Strana

Hotel Kampa★★

Všehrdova 16
Tram 9, 12 or 22, stop: Újezd
☎ 257 32 05 08
☏ 257 32 02 62
www.prague-hotel.wz.cz/
hotel-kampa
Double room off-season
Kč4,000, peak season Kč5,500.

Wonderfully located in a peaceful side street, this 17th-century Baroque building was a former armory. The hotel was renovated in 1922 and has 85 rooms with shower. Some have superb views over Kampa Park and the river. The restaurant is open 7am-10pm. On sunny days you can sit outside and enjoy a relaxing drink or meal.

Hotel Neruda

Nerudova 44
Tram 12, 20 or 22, stop:
Malostranské náměstí
☎ 257 53 55 57
☏ 257 53 14 92
Double room off-season
Kč7,500, peak season Kč8,500, weekend rates available.
www.hotelneruda-praha.cz

Located on the route leading to the Castle, the Neruda hotel's 20 rooms are set in a magnificent 1348 building, beautifully restored in a mixture of classic and modern styles. Located in the heart of the tourist area, you will enjoy its peaceful atmosphere, its interior patio and its small café overlooking the street.

Pension Dientzenhofer★★

Nosticova 2
Tram 12 or 22, stop:
Malostranské náměstí
☎ 257 311 319
☏ 257 320 888
www.dientzenhofer.cz
Double room off-season from Kč2,800, peak season from Kč3,800.

The architect Kilian Dientzenhofer was born in this 15th-century building, which has only six rooms, so you do need to make a reservation well in advance. Located near Charles Bridge, it's in a quiet residential area, and in summer you can eat breakfast in the garden overlooking the lovely Kampa Park.

U Raka Hotel

Černínská 10
Tram 22
☎ 220 51 11 00
☎ 233 355 804
Double room from Kč5,600 to Kč6,800 depending on the season.

Located in the Nový Svět district, this pension is housed in a half-timbered house. The seven rooms are comfortable, and you'll have a quiet stay. Note that children are not allowed.

U Páva★★★★

U Lužického semináře 32
Metro Malostranská, tram 12 or 22 stop: Malostranské náměstí
☎ 257 533 573
F 257 530 484
www.athos.cz/hotel-u-pava
Double room from Kč4,300 to Kč6,000 depending on the season.

This charming hotel is located almost on the banks of the Vltava near the Charles Bridge, which makes it quite expensive. It has a wonderful view of the Castle and a restaurant with excellent fish dishes. The rooms are comfortable and spacious.

Hotel Hoffmeister★★★★

Pod Bruskou 7
Metro Malostranská
☎ 251 01 71 11
☎ 251 017 120
www.hoffmeister.cz
Double room off-season Kč5,800, peak season Kč7,800.

This large, modern, luxury hotel was designed by the son of Adolf Hoffmeister, a friend of Picasso and the French surrealists. The 43 rooms are tastefully decorated and well

worth the extra cost, if this is what you're looking for.

U Karlova Mostu★★

Na Kampě 15
Tram 12 or 22, stop: Malostrasnké nám.
☎ 257 531 430
☎ 257 531 431
Double room off-season Kč4,000, peak season Kč5,600.

Located on Kampa island, this former historic 15th-century brewery has undergone refurbishment and is now a magnificent hotel on the banks of the Vltava, offering several attic rooms, a restaurant with a small garden and an old-fashioned brasserie.

U Krale Karla

Neruda – Úvoz 4
Tram 12 or 22, stop: Malostranské nám.
☎ 257 531 211
☎ 257 531 049
www.romantichotels.cz
Double room from Kč3,900 to Kč5,500 depending on the season.

Set in two beautifully restored houses, linked by a narrow, brightly lit courtyard, this is a quiet and refined hotel. The bedrooms, with their painted wood ceilings, stained-glass windows, wooden furniture and fireplaces, are spacious and sophisticated – some even have wonderful views over the Castle.

The restaurant and breakfast room are just as elegant.

Staré Město (Old Town)

Betlém Club

Betlémské nám. 9
Metro Národní třída
☎ 222 221 574
☎ 222 221 575
www.bethlemclub.cz
Double room from Kč2,900 to Kč3,900 depending on the season.

Ideally located on Bethlehem Square near several cafés and restaurants, this pension has 20 small rooms at reasonable prices. Enjoy your breakfast in an authentic Gothic cellar.

Hotel Evropa

Vaclavské namesti 25
Metro Mustek or Museum
☎ 224.215.387
☎ 224.224.544
www.evropahotel.cz
Double room from Kč1,430 (without bathroom) to Kč3,000 depending on the season.

Built in 1889 and refurbished in the art nouveau style between 1903 and 1905, the Evropa hotel remains one of the architectural jewels of the city. Its renowned café and restaurant remain true to their reputation. Even though some of the rooms are very basic and others in urgent need of repainting, the whole building is still full of charm.

Riverside Hotel★★★

Janackovo nabrezi 15
Metro Andel; tram 9, 12, 20
☎ 225 994 611
✆ 225 994 622
www.riversideprague.com
Double room off-season
Kč6,300, peak season Kč7,500,
weekend reductions.

Located in a peaceful district on the banks of the Vltava, this charming hotel is a true symbol of elegance. The refined interior design, created by Pascale de Montrémy, is a subtle combination of colors and space, cleverly bringing together tradition and modernism. The staff is attentive and extends a warm welcome; the bedrooms are spacious – some have a terrace – and offer unusual views over the town.

U Staré paní

Michalská 9
Metro Můstek
☎ 224 228 090
✆ 224 226 659
www.ustarepani.cz
Double room from Kč3,000 to
Kč4,300 depending on the
season.

This hotel is ideally located and has recently been renovated. It has 18 clean, comfortable rooms, and the jazz club in the basement has an excellent program.

Hotel Mejstrik★★★

Jakubska 5
Metro Nám. Republiky
☎ 224 800 055
✆ 224 800 856
www.hotelmejjstrik.cz
Double room from Kč4,400 to
Kč6,200 depending on the
season.

Near the town hall, this hotel which has been completely refurbished is a little jewel of art nouveau, an exceptional building where interior decoration and furniture are in perfect harmony. The 27 rooms and the two suites are particularly elegant, the restaurant truly fabulous – and the welcome is very warm.

Hotel U Krále Jiřího (King George Hotel)

Liliová 10
Metro Staroměstská
☎ 224 248 797
www.athos.cz/hotel-u-krale-jiriho
Double room from Kč3,000
depending on the season.

This 14th-century building

has only eight rooms, some located in the attic. It is simply decorated and its greatest attribute is its central location near Charles Bridge.

Pension Unitas

Bartolomějská 9
Metro Národní třída
☎ 224 221 802
✆ 224 217 555
www.unitas.cz
Double room from Kč1,200 from
Kč2,000 depending on the
season.

This house used to be a Jesuit monastery and then a prison for political prisoners, where the secret police conducted their interrogations. Václav Havel was once held in cell number six in the basement. It is now a peaceful pension where you'll find yourself in the quiet company of the Franciscan sisters.

Hotel U Klenotníka (The Goldsmith's Hotel)

Rytířská 3
Metro Můstek
☎ 224 21 16 99
✆ 224 22 10 25
Double room from Kč3,200 to
Kč3,700.

Conveniently located between Wenceslas Square and the Old Town Square, this family-run pension has a lovely restaurant and 11 very comfortable rooms. In former years it was a jewelry factory.

Hotel Josef★★

Rybná 20
Metro Nám. Republiky
☎ 221 700 111
✆ 221 700 999
www.hoteljosef.com
Double room from Kč5,000 to
Kč6,500 depending on the
season.

Created by the Czech interior designer Eva Jiřičná, in pure high-tech style, the Josef Hotel, all steel and glass, first opened in 2002 and quickly established itself as one of Prague's most distinguished hotels.

Nové Město (New Town)

Hotel 16 (U sv Kateřiny)★★★

Kateřinská 16
Metro Karlovo náměstí
☎ 224 91 96 76
✆ 224 920 626
Double room from Kč3,500.

Just a ten-minute walk from Wenceslas Square and close to the Botanical Gardens, this hotel is in an ideal location. It has been entirely renovated and has suites, double rooms and single rooms, one of which has facilities for the disabled.

1 - Hotel 16
2 - Hotel Josef
3 - Hotel U Klenotníka
4 - Hotel Mejstrik

All the rooms are quiet and comfortable, and some have small lounges to relax in at the end of the day.

Mercure

Na Poříčí 7
Metro Náměstí Republiky, line B
☎ 221 800 800
☏ 221 800 801
www.mercure.com
Double room from Kč3,000 to Kč6,900 depending on the season.

The impressive Mercure hotel has a gourmet restaurant and a well-stocked wine cellar. Located in the town center, next to the Municipal House.

Vinohrady

Hotel Anna

Budečská 17
Metro Náměstí Míru
☎ 222 51 31 11
☏ 222 51 51 58
www.hotelanna.cz
Double room Kč3,400.

This hotel has 23 single and double rooms and is in a quiet area close to the center. The hotel has a bar with a terrace open from 5-11pm.

Luník

Londýnská 50
Metro I.P. Pavlova
☎ 224 25 39 74
☏ 224 25 39 86
www.hotel-lunik.cz
Double room from Kč2,320 to Kč3,300 depending on the season.

This is a modernized hotel in a good location, just 15 minutes' walk or two metro stops from Wenceslas Square. There are 35 quiet rooms at reasonable prices, which are all extremely clean if a little small. Recently renovated, the hotel is in excellent condition and has a simple but attractive decor.

Hotel Sibelius

Jana Masaryka 39 - Prague 2
☎ 222 521 700
☏ 222 521 701
www.oktours.cz/sibelius
Apartment for two Kč2,700.

In the past, this residential area (Vinohrady) consisted only of vineyards planted by Charles IV. A stone's throw from the last remaining vine stocks, stands a gleaming apartment building in shades of ocher, adorned with stucco cherubs. From the reception to the bedrooms and even the elevator, everything is luxurious. There are 12 apartments with small kitchens for two or four people. Great price given the setting and the location, ten minutes from the town center by tram.

Restaurants

1 - Švejk
2 - Hanavský Pavilon
3 - Country Life
4 - Vinárna v zátiší

Malá Strana

Hanavský Pavilon★

Letenské sady 173
Tram 18, 22, stop:
Hodovkovysordy, then Gogolova
Street as far as the park
☎ 233 323 641
Every day 10am-11pm; terrace
Apr.-Sep. every day 11am-11pm.

Located in Letná Park, this restaurant is decorated in the Baroque and Rococo styles and resembles a hunting lodge. The view of Prague is magnificent, the atmosphere peaceful and the service extremely attentive.

U Maltézských rytířů★★★

Prokopská 10
Tram 12, 22, stop: Malostranské nám.
☎ 257 530 075
Every day 1-11pm.

Dine by candlelight in this intimate restaurant close to the French embassy. Choose a table on the first floor or in the Romanesque basement. The food is good value, with a choice of local and international dishes. Make sure you try the apple strudel (jablkový závin).

U Kocoura★★

Nerudova 2
Tram 12, 22 stop:
Malostranské nám.
☎ 257 53 01 07
Every day 11am-11pm.

This is the place to taste the best *Pilsner Urquell* beer in Prague while enjoying local dishes of sausages and cheese specially concocted to complement the beer.

Staré Město

Švejk★

Široká 20
Metro Staroměstská
☎ 222 311 199
or 224 813 964
Every day 11am-11pm.

Named after the famous soldier Švjek (see p. 17) whose ruddy, jovial face is part of the decor, this traditional restaurant offers excellent Czech cuisine. Photographs, posters and old-fashioned ads, stained-glass windows showing simple *hospoda* scenes, wood paneling and wooden tables make for a friendly atmosphere.

Country Life★★

Melantrichova 15
Michalská 18
Metro Můstek
☎ 224 213 373
et 224 213 366
Sun. 11am-8pm, Mon.-Thu.
9am-7.30pm, Fri. 9am-5pm.

This is a great restaurant for vegetarians and vegans, tucked away in a pretty courtyard; in fact at one time it was almost Prague's only vegetarian restaurant. The salads, soups, hot dishes and desserts, all with Eastern European touches, are delicious. Don't miss the beetroot soup (*boršč*).

Universal★

V Jirchářích 6
Metro Národní třída
☎ 224 934 416
Every day 11.30am-1am.

Excellent French cooking, great variety, good value for money. Everything is delicious, the ingredients are top-quality: a gourmet meal for an extremely reasonable price.

Kogo Ristorante★

Havelská 27
Metro Můstek
☎ 224 214 543
Every day 11am-11pm.

This restaurant offers delicious, beautifully presented Italian cuisine. There are two rooms to choose from on either side of the corridor: on the right, a huge room with a modern and bright design, on the left, a more intimate room. Warm welcome and large meals.

Vinárna v zátiší★★★

Liliová 1
Metro Národní třída or Můstek
☎ 222 22 06 27
Every day noon-3pm, 5.30-11pm.

If you're looking for the perfect place for a romantic meal, then look no further. Candlelit dinner in a sophisticated and peaceful atmosphere, with excellent and discreet service, is the order of the day. The dishes are original but inspired by Czech, French and international cuisines. The food is beautifully presented and wine can be bought by the glass. Make a reservation in advance.

Francouzská restaurace★★★

Náměstí Republiky 5
Metro Náměstí Republiky
☎ 222 00 27 70
☎ 222 00 27 78
Every day noon-4pm and 6-11pm.

This wonderful art-nouveau restaurant has an excellent selection of traditional dishes together with some delicious French food. The prices are very reasonable and the atmosphere welcoming. Treat yourself to a night out if you're only in Prague for a short time. Make a reservation in advance.

Plzenska restaurace★★

Náměstí Republiky 5
Metro náměstí Republiky

☎ 222 00 27 80
Every day 11am-11pm.

In the basement of the Municipal House there's a large *hospoda*, decorated with painted wood and ceramics. Choose from some delicious traditional dishes served in a friendly atmosphere. You may be treated to a few strains of the accordion. This is one of the best examples of the *hospoda*.

Pivnice u Pivrnce★

Maiselova 3
Metro Staroměstská
☎ 222 329 404
Every day 11am-midnight.

This pub is in the basement and is decorated with some amusing cartoons. You may not always appreciate the humor of the frescoes, which are rather saucy. The cuisine is simple and traditional, the atmosphere relaxed, particularly at the end of a night spent sampling the beer cellar!

Lary Fary★★

Dlouha 30
Metro Náměstí Republiky
☎ 222 320 154
Every day 11am-midnight.

Huge delicious kebabs come straight onto your plate! This American restaurant offers a cuisine inspired by flavors from all over the world, in a refined

modern setting with a subtly exotic atmosphere. U Rumpálu is an original and relaxed place to eat.

U Dvou Koček★★

Uhelný trh 10
Metro Můstek or Národní třída
☎ 224 22 99 82
Every day 11am-11pm.

This 17th-century tavern has become rather touristy, but it still manages to retain its warm, friendly atmosphere thanks to the accordion players who add a certain something to your meal (and your check). The food is simple and excellent value.

U Vejvodů★★

Jilská 4
Metro Narodní třída
☎ 224 219 999
www.restauraceuvejvodu.cz
Every day 10am-2am.

The latest Czech establishment to offer local cuisine and the convivial atmosphere of a big tavern. A huge vat is suspended above the bar on the first floor, where the beer flows freely. Expect to pay around Kč55 for the fixed-price menu, KŤ80-240 otherwise.

Barock★

Pařížská 24
Metro Staroměstská
☎ 222 329 221
Every day 10am-1am.

Chandeliers, mirrors and columns give the finishing touch to this designer bar. The modern decor (even the bathroom is worth a visit!) provides a colorful, attractive setting to enjoy sushi and sashimi, refined fusion cuisine and delicious desserts. Everything is beautifully presented and served with a choice of very good wines. The small room at the back is more intimate.

Nové Město

Dynamo

Pštrosova 29
Metro Národní třída
or Karlovo náměstí
☎ 224 932 020
Mon.-Sun. 11.30am-midnight.

The futuristic, very stylized interior decor was created by Olgoj Chorchoi and Ales Najbrt, two young Czech designers. On the light green walls are displayed works by Andy Warhol, and the laminated wooden furniture stands next to items of a very modern design. International cuisine at very affordable prices.

Novoměstský Pivovar★★

Vodičkova 20
Metro Karlovo náměstí, Muzeum or Můstek
☎ 222 232 448
Mon.-Fri. 10am-11.30pm,
Sat. 11.30am-11.30pm, Sun. noon-10pm.

This maze of beer halls has become very popular due to the excellent Czech food served here. On the menu is a delicious pork knuckle dish (vepřové pečené koleno), and the portions are very generous. To complement the tasty food try a glass of the beer, which is made on the premises. There's a friendly atmosphere, but prices have been raised due to its increased popularity. Always make a reservation.

Restaurace pivovarský dům★★★

Ječná/Lípova 15
Metro Karlovo náměstí
☎ 296 21 66 66
Every day 11am-11.30pm.

Good Czech food served in a setting dedicated to the art of beer-making. The light beer is brewed in the basement of the building and is naturally cloudy. Ask for a tour of the interesting brewery. The dishes are good value (Kč55-90) and the portions generous. The location is also excellent and it is very difficult to make a choice between this restaurant and Novomžstskž Pivovar, so why not try them both.

U Rozvařilů★

Na Poříčí 26
Metro Náměstí Republiky or Florenc
Mon.-Fri. 8am-7.30pm,
Sat. 9am-7pm, Sun. 10am-5pm.

You can still find snack bars in Prague (bufet or samoobsluha), and they serve excellent meals that are quick and good value. Take your pick from sandwiches or hot dishes, and then decide whether to eat standing up, as regulars tend to, or at a table. If you're hungry and in a rush, this is an ideal spot and a favorite haunt of the locals.

U Rumpálu★★★

Školská 14
Metro Karlovo náměstí, Můstek or Muzeum
☎ 222 23 10 44.
Every day 11am-midnight.

This basement restaurant has a French feel, with wooden tables and benches and pretty tablecloths. The food, however, is very Czech and includes some light dishes and a good salad bar.

1 - Restaurace pivovarský
dům
2 - Barock
3 - Dynamo
4 - Barock

Ztráty A Nálezy★★

Žitná 15
Metro Karlovo náměstí,
Můstek or Muzeum
☎ 222 233 915
Every day 11am-11pm.

A regular haunt for locals, where there's always a warm welcome from the hospitable owner. The food is traditional Czech, with wholesome winter soups and some unusual dishes. On a sunny day you can eat in the garden. The lunch menu is Kč60-70 and the evening menu Kč150.

Skořepka★★

Skořepka 1
Metro Můstek or Narodní třida
☎ 224 21 47 15
Every day noon-midnight.

A pleasant, country-style inn decorated with wood, old tools and a real plow. The tasty local cuisine includes a number of traditional recipes. The fixed-price menu is around Kč69, otherwise between Kč150 and Kč200.

U Čížků ★★★

Karlovo náměstí 34
Metro Karlovo náměstí
☎ 222 23 22 57
Mon.-Fri. 9.30am-10pm,
Sat.-Sun. 11am-10pm.

This restaurant, with its velvet wall hangings and tapestry, serves traditional Czech food. Meat, game and fish are on the menu, and the food is tasty and quite light. Plzeň beer is served and reservations are advisable.

Vinohrady

Tiger Tiger★★

Anny Letenské 5
Metro Námĕstí Miru
☎ 222 51 20 84
Mon.-Fri. 11am-11pm,
Sat.-Sun. 5-11pm.

Why not enjoy authentic Thai cuisine in Prague? Here is a brand-new address to tease your taste buds with pork curry in coconut milk, red fish curry and other delicious dishes at reasonable prices.

Černá Kočka Bilý Kocour★★

Vinohradská 62
Metro Jiřího z Poděbrad
☎ 224 257 626
Mon.-Fri. 11.30am-1am,
Sat.-Sun. 4pm-1am.

Located in the basement, this bar and restaurant is mainly patronized by young Czechs. Wooden floors, light wood paneling and furniture combine to create a welcoming interior, softly lit by an orange light. You can eat salads, pasta, meat and fish, as well as many cocktails.

Tearooms, cafés
and pastry shops

1 - Kaaba kavarna
2 - Cafe Imperial
3 - Kavárna Obecní Dům
4 - Cafe Imperial

Malá Strana

Kavárna Chimera

Lázeňská 6
Tram 12, 22 stop:
Malostranské nám.
☎ 606 321 967
Every day noon-midnight.

This art gallery-cum-café is a favorite haunt of young people, with furniture in different colors and comfortable sofas; and works of contemporary Czech artists on the walls. The atmosphere is welcoming. You can have pastries, toast or more substantial snacks.

U zeleného čaje

Nerudova 19
Tram 12, 22 stop: Malostranské nám.
☎ 257 53 00 27
Every day 11am-10pm.

The "Green Tea" is a great little café to stop at for refreshments in the heart of the tourist area. It has a beautiful view onto Nerudova and a large selection of teas (green, black or herbal). There are also some homemade delicacies served on the local blue and white ceramic plates. It's a cozy place to go in winter.

Staré Město

Cafe Imperial

Na Porici 15
Metro Nám. Republiky
☎ 222 316 012
Mon.-Sat. 9am-midnight,
Sun. 9am-11pm.

In this wonderful café full of nostalgic reminiscences of the times of the First Republic, waiters dressed in black and white race through a forest of ceramic colonnades. Coffee is served with a free dumpling. Jazz concerts on Thursdays, Fridays and Saturdays at 9pm.

Café Divadlo na zábradlí

Aneñské náměstí 5
Metro Staroměstská
☎ 222 868 860
Mon.-Fri. 10am-1am, Sat.-Sun. 4pm-1am; closed Jul. and Aug.

Located on the attractive Anenské Square, this café belongs

to the famous Prague Theater. The mime artist Ladislav Fialka, a pupil of Marcel Marceau, and Václav Havel, then a stagehand, both came here. There are dedications to Czech actors on the walls and a small inner terrace. When you leave the café, take the little Stříbrná Street with its uneven cobble-stones and winding route.

Cremeria Milano

Parizska 20
Metro Staroměstská
☎ 224 811 010
Every day 10am-11pm.

On the most elegant avenue in Prague, this Italian ice-cream parlor sells a wide selection of ice cream to take out or eat in. At the back, you can enjoy cakes and ice creams in a small, richly decorated tearoom (their hot chocolate is delicious).

the Internet. You'll see elderly ladies and tourists looking somewhat overwhelmed, and it's a wonderful place to just sit and watch the world go by. Breakfast is served from 7.30am to 11am, and main meals are served throughout the day.

Týnská literární kavárna

Týnská 6
Metro Můstek, Staroměstská or Náměstí Republiky
☎ 224 827 807
Mon.-Fri. 9am-11pm,
Sat.-Sun. 10am-11pm.

This café is linked to the bookstore next door and has a lovely terrace in a quiet courtyard. It's a stone's throw from the Old Town, just beside Týn Courtyard (see p. 57), and has a selection of simple but tasty dishes.

(see p. 57)

Kavárna Obecní Dům

Náměstí Republiky 5
Metro Náměstí Republiky
☎ 222 002 763
Every day 7.30am-11pm.

The Municipal House café has an appropriately majestic art-nouveau interior. It's all crystal, chrome and mirrors, with waiters in uniform and piano music in the background. There's also a small booth (salónek) where you can access

Odkolek

Rytířská 12
Metro Můstek
Mon.-Fri. 7am-8pm,
Sat. 8am-8pm, Sun. 10am-8pm.

This is an ideal spot to enjoy traditional Czech pastries for breakfast. The decor is blue and white with natural wood. People start to stand in line at 7pm for the unsold cakes, which are then reduced by 30 percent. Order and pay at the counter before taking a seat.

Nové Město

Café Louvre

Národní třída 20
☎ 224 930 949
Galerie Louvre
☎ 224 931 565
Every day 8am-11.30pm.

Once the haunt of a group of intellectuals, including Kafka and his friend Max Brod, this café was closed under the Communist regime and converted into offices. It has now been restored, and its doors are open once again. The waiters wear white aprons and bow ties, and the service is impeccable. Enjoy a coffee and cake while taking the opportunity to read the inter-national papers.

Kaaba kavarna

Manesova 20
Metro Muzeum
☎ 222 254 021
Mon.-Sat. 8am-10pm,
Sun. 10am-10pm.

This small café doubles up as a grocery store and is a truly magical place: the white ceilings and walls are criss-crossed with thick colorful geometric lines, the furniture and lights date back to the 1950s. You can enjoy delicious coffees from all over the world – the *Jamaican Blue Mountain* is truly wonderful.

Platýz

Narodní 37 (in the passageway)
Metro Národní třída
☎ 224 211 161
Mon.-Fri. 10am-11pm,
Sat.-Sun. 11am-11pm.

If on a warm sunny day you feel like treating yourself to a sweet or savory snack on a terrace, come to this large café located close to the Tesco store. The tea here is particularly recommended.

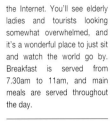

Practicalities

Although on many levels Prague does not match some of the other European capitals, it still has much more to offer than the ubiquitous specialties such as crystal and garnet. The Czechs are excellent craftspeople, have a real taste for music and are very creative when it comes to fashion and design. As you stroll along, you might even come across a rare item in a secondhand bookstore or antiques store. Forget the image of a provincial town, Prague is a 21st-century capital.

Opening hours

The smaller shops are usually open from 8-9am until 5-6pm, closing at 4pm on Fridays. Most of the larger stores are open Monday through Friday and until 1pm on Saturday. However, there is a certain flexibility to these times, and you may find stores closed for no apparent reason during normal opening hours. The stores in the main centers are adapting their hours to the needs of the tourists, and they now remain open until at least 7pm, with no break for lunch. Markets in Prague open early on weekdays but their closing times vary. You'll find that the stores are often very crowded on Saturdays and that it's easier to wander from store to store during the week, when there are noticeably fewer people around.

Where to shop

You'll find souvenir and gift shops in the main tourist areas, including the route from the Old Town Square to the Castle, via Karlova and the Charles Bridge. Prices can vary dramatically from shop to shop. It's important to make a few comparisons before you actually buy anything. If you are looking for food or clothes, head for the lower end of Charles Square, around Národní třída, or in the area near the popular Tesco store. Other good spots include Železná Street and Celetná, near the Old Town Square. The best areas to head for on Sundays include Charles Square, Na příkopě, Železná,

Národní třída and the streets around the Old Town Square. The Little Quarter is a good spot for weekend shopping also. Most of the Czech shops and stores which sell foreign label goods are open on Saturdays and Sundays until 5pm.

How to bargain

You'll usually find that goods have price tags attached, though this is frequently not the case in antique shops and secondhand bookstores. If an item has no price tag, then feel free to bargain. There are several methods, but the most simple and effective tactic is to ask the opening price, and then appear shocked. Gradually negotiate a more reasonable price, and you may find you're able to reduce the original by as much as 25 percent. Your success will depend upon your patience and acting ability!

How to pay

Credit cards are gradually becoming more acceptable in Prague, but do check the stickers on the door of the store, restaurant or hotel first. To be sure ask before you have your meal or commit yourself to a purchase. Your signature will be closely checked against your card,

so take extra care when signing. If your card is lost or stolen, call:
MasterCard and EuroCard
☎ 261 354 649
Visa and Diner's Club
☎ 224 125 353
Diner's Club
☎ 267 197 450
American Express
☎ 222 800 111

Sales and bargains

Sales (*sleva*) are becoming more popular with the arrival of Western stores. Clothes, shoes and accessories are often sold at good reductions (up to 50 percent from the end of August until September or October). Some sales start after New Year.

Customs regulations

You can import 90 liters of wine, 10 liters of spirits, 400 cigarettes and 400 cigars free of tax into another EU country. If you buy an old item, it would be better if the invoice stated "item less than 50 years old."

Shipping

If you buy a heavy item, such as a piece of furniture, you can arrange for it to be transported home. The price is

FINDING YOUR WAY

Many stores now have websites where you can usually find detailed directions and often a map of how to get there. You may also be able to browse the products available online.

generally fixed and is based on volume. You'll need a photocopy of your passport, a photocopy of the invoice, a document confirming that you're a tourist in Prague, a certificate from the store and a document showing the list of your purchases and the total amount paid. You should always keep the invoice.You may be asked to show it at customs, and you'll find it useful if you decide to sell your item in the future. It will also be needed for insurance purposes in the event of theft.
Contact AGS Prague to arrange transport worldwide:
Na Prosecké
vyhlídce 3/807
☎ 286 882 160
✆ 286 882 161

Women's
fashion

Continuing the tradition of the famous Prague fashion houses of the 1930s, some young Czech designers have developed original designer clothes labels which have no connection to the gray and shapeless "uniforms" of the Communist era. So, next to the famous foreign brands, you can now find Czech shops which display very creative collections by playing with the subtlety of shape and color.

Klara Nademlynská
Dlouha 7
☎ 224 818 769
Mon.-Fri. 10am-7pm,
Sat. 11am-6pm.

In a pretty shop with elegant bright pink walls, this fashionable designer offers an original collection of clothes and accessories. Her flowing, colorful and extremely feminine creations are subdued and elegant, sometimes even unusual. You'll find evening dresses, as well as pleated skirts and stripy blouses, printed cottons, colored silks and knitwear.

Ivana Follova
Vodičkova 36
☎ 296 236 497
Mon.-Sat. 10.30am-7pm.

Silk, velvet, linen, *crepe de Chine*, Ivana Follova makes use of the most beautiful and most comfortable materials to create a sober and elegant range of clothes suitable for any occasion. This small shop is truly an Aladdin's cave and you can also find beautiful jewelry, scarves and hats, not to mention attractive ties for the men.

Le Boheme

Štupartská 7
☎ 224 827 379
Mon.-Fri. 10am-7pm,
Sat. 10am-5pm.

This shop has retained the warm welcome which used to be the characteristic of sewing stores and dressmakers' workshops of the past. People come here to look for unusual designs of plain or printed linen dresses, blouses, comfortable sweaters and corduroy coats. Prices are reasonable and you can even have some garments custom-made.

MarLen

Karoliny Svetlé 12
☎ 224 236 728
Mon.-Fri. 9am-6pm.

The number of different materials you can find in this shop is truly impressive.

Silks or woolen materials, handpainted materials and batiks can all be found, from the shelves to the shopwindow or on the furniture. This is the ideal opportunity to look for a piece of material (from Kč800 per meter/yard) to make yourself a dress unlike anybody else's. The woolen materials, handwoven, a blend of silk and mohair, are really superb.

Timoure

V Kolkovne 6
☎ 222 327 358
Mon.-Fri. 10am-7pm,
Sat. 11am-5pm.

Alexandra Pavalova's and Ivana Safrankova's creations are like their shop: simple, elegant and comfortable. Their clothes – particularly stylish pantsuits – are both classical and modern, mixing cleverly

colors and materials. Their collection is very fresh, just as attractive and irresistible as their pretty fitting rooms.

Siluet Mode

Široká 15
☎ 603 418 238
Mon.-Fri. 10am-7pm,
Sat.-Sun. 11am-6pm.

This is a distinctive collection, mainly comprising extremely elegant evening dresses. Eva Plzakova loves to work with beautiful materials, particularly silk, and this is very noticeable. She also makes simple yet unusual accessories and jewelry which she sells at very affordable prices (starting at Kč500).

Boheme

Dusni 8
☎ 224 813 840
Mon.-Fri. 11am-8pm,
Sat. 11am-5pm.

Hana Stocklassa's objective is clear: clothes must be above all comfortable, wearable for any occasion and you should be able to mix and match them with other labels. You'll find the basic range of handknitted sweaters and cardigans, and also leather or suede skirts and pants. A real "Bohemian" look that can be completed with bags and necklaces.

GALERIE MÓDY – HELENA FEJKOVA

Helena Fejkova's haute couture and leisurewear collections are on display in a huge and elegant gallery in the splendid Lucerna Palace (see p. 61). Her creations, made out of natural materials like wool and linen, are characterized by pure, simple lines and great attention to detail. You can also find creations by other associate designers, as well as original accessories and jewelry by Zuzana Sléhová among others. The gallery also houses a charming little café with a magnificent view over the art-nouveau features of the building.

Štěpánská 61; ☎ 224 211 514
Mon.-Fri. 10am-7pm, Sat. 10am-3pm.

Men's fashion

We have to admit it, when it comes to fashion, men have less choice than women. However, although there are still relatively few Czech fashion designers, foreign labels fill the gap. This is an ideal opportunity to find some clothes which may not be extremely original but are good quality and fashionable. So the men get a chance to go window-shopping, too.

Jozef Sloboda

Na příkopě 12, Černá Růže (level 2)
☎ 221 014 408
Every day 11am-7pm.

This young Czech designer offers a fresh and original range of clothes. The cuts, finishing touches (pockets, buttons and zippers) and sometimes rather unusual colors, are of high quality, always designed with originality without being over-exuberant. This is an ideal shop to find an unusual pair of jeans, a jacket or a T-shirt. The shirts, very elegant though more classic, can be worn with whatever you like. The women's fashion section is just as creative.

Diegle

Na příkopě 16
☎ 22402160502
Mon.-Fri. 10am-8pm, Sat. 10am-7pm, Sun. 11am-7pm.

This elegant shop with its refined interior decor displays the collection by German designer Diegle and Eterna, a specialist in men's fashion with sober and classical lines. The welcoming and attentive staff will guide you in your choice among the wide range of suits, shirts, sweaters and polo shirts. You can select from many accessories to put the finishing touch to your outfit, particularly from beautiful silk or satin scarves and ties.

Stones

28 Října 2
☎ 224 237 804
Mon.-Fri. 10am-8pm, Sat. 10am-7pm, Sun. 11am-6pm.

This fairly classic range of ready-to-wear clothes is aimed at a young and modern clientele that wishes to follow fashion without appearing excessively different or extravagant. Suits, shirts and accessories are plain and elegant with just enough color or patterns to remain fashionable.

Adam Steiner

Václavské nám. 24
☎ 224 220 594
Mon.-Fri. 9am-7pm,
Sat. 10am-6pm.

It's worth coming into this shop to experience the quiet atmosphere of one of the great Prague tailors and you could be tempted to get a suit custom-made (at the back of the shop). Their ready-to-wear range is in a classical, sober and refined style. Sportswear

now takes up a large part of the display, with a whole aisle devoted entirely to golf, from outfits to equipment.

Kenvelo

Václavské nám. 1
☎ 221 111 711
Mon.-Sat. 9am-9pm,
Sun. 10am-9pm.

Created in 1989, this Czech brand can be found everywhere in Prague and in the rest of the country. Appealing to the young, the shops are modern (almost always packed) and the shelves are laden with fashionable clothes (jeans, T-shirts and jackets) at really attractive prices. Succumb to temptation and

bring back a sweatshirt with the now famous white silk K on it.

O. P. Prostějov

Vodičkova 33
☎ 224 946 129
Mon.-Fri. 10am-7pm,
Sat. 10am-2pm.

A benchmark in Czech ready-to-wear, this well-established label can be found almost everywhere in Prague today, and is much appreciated for the quality of its flannel, woolen or cotton suits. Prostějof is gradually modernizing but mainly produces two- or three-piece suits in discreet colors (black, navy blue and charcoal gray). Prices remain reasonable and you can buy Czech-made ties.

ALIEN TATTOO & BODY PIERCING

At the end of the corridor, go up to the second floor. If you have made up your mind, you might come out of here with a piercing or a tattoo, wearing a suede jacket, "rave style" glasses on top of your head, yellow pants and a 100 percent pink nylon shirt. To complete the image you should also be playing techno or pop tunes on your MP3 player and carrying enough dyes to turn your hair any color of the rainbow. While you are here you can also find out about the next "in" evening, just to show off your new look!

Jilská 22, 1st floor; ☎ 224 235 766
Mon.-Sat. 11am-7pm, Sun. 1-6pm.

Next

Pasaz Myslbek, Na Přikopě 19/21
☎ 224 232 230
Mon.-Fri. 9.30am-8pm,
Sat. 9am-7pm, Sun. 11am-6pm.

The very trendy Pasaz Mylsbek is home to one of the shops selling the famous British brand. As in London, come and shop here and you'll go away with fashionable, good-quality clothes, underwear or accessories, whose prices are always attractive as there are often special offers to be found.

Hats, shoes
and leather goods

Prague follows fashion and what would fashion be without the many accessories necessary to create your own look? Although you'll find them in almost all clothes shops, there are also plenty of "specialized" shops, centered mainly on Wenceslas Square. And on the subject of fashion, you can find absolutely everything you want here, from the most unusual hats to the most extravagant shoes.

Kreibich

Michalská 14
☎ 224 222 522
www.kreibich.cz
Mon.-Fri. 10am-6pm,
Sat.-Sun. 10am-5pm.

If you get caught out by the Bohemian winter and if you are shivering with cold despite drinking mulled wine and

Becherovka, Robert Kreibich may be able to help cheer you up. With his family, in his workshop just below the shop, he transforms lambskins from Spain, rats' skins from Canada and Czech chinchillas into elegant (and warm!) *chapkas*, gloves, mittens, coats, fur-lined jackets, and more. There's a vast choice of colors. Discounts in the summer. Animal lovers will find synthetic and much cheaper *chapkas* on the stalls in Karlova Street.

Delmas

Vodičkova 36
☎ 296 236 923
Mon.-Fri. 9.30am-8pm, Sat. 10am-7.30pm, Sun. 10am-6pm.

Do you want to buy an accessory? Then hurry to this shop where you'll find Czech-made purses inspired by Italian fashion. Depending on the seasons, colors can be bright (yellow, blue, green or orange) or more discreet (brown, black or patent), and shapes can be classic or modern. Prices are reasonable (Kč1,500 to Kč3,500) and the finish perfect.

Galex

Maiselova 12
☎ 222 329 006
Mon.-Fri. 10am-7pm,
Sat.-Sun. 10am-5pm.

This small shop located at the corner of Maiselova Street and

Vezenska Street, in the heart of the old Jewish district, only sells Czech-made products – except for shoes. Purses, wallets, gloves, hats, belts and clothes are classic but of very good quality.

Hedva

Na příkopě 16
☎ 224 212 566
Mon.-Fri. 10am-6pm.

As if lost among the most fashionable stores, this quaint little shop puts up a brave fight. The welcome is extremely warm and the staff will not hesitate to show you a wide choice of classic, locally made silk ties and bow ties, at very reasonable prices. To put the finishing touch to your outfit, you may be tempted by a pair of cuff links, a tie clip or an umbrella.

Ecco

Na Příkopě 7
☎ 224 239 964
Mon.-Sat. 10am-8pm,
Sun. 11am-7pm.

The stated mission of Ecco is that that you should feel good in your body. Ecco designs shoes for people "on the

move," whatever your activity or sport may be. This modern and bright store offers a very varied range of shoes. The town shoes, sober and elegant, are rather uninspiring, whereas the sports and outdoor shoes are more imaginative and colorful. You can also find socks and some well-made and attractive leather goods here.

The Art

Národní 36
☎ 224 948 828
Mon.-Fri. 9.30am-7pm,
Sat. 9.30am-5pm,
Sun. 10am-5pm.

It is certainly an "art" to be able to bring together in the same store such diverse styles. Apart from some leather clothes and accessories, you'll find mainly shoes here, and not just any shoes. Of course, there are some classic ranges, but the store mainly offers "New Rock" shoes, that is boots and ankle boots, with platform soles and countless buckles and laces. As for colors, although black is dominant, why not go for a really bright purple?

Vagabond

28 Října 10
☎ 222 244 927
Mon.-Fri. 9am-8pm, Sat.
9am-6.30pm, Sun. 10am-6pm.

The famous Swedish brand sells shoes and plain leisurewear boots. Comfortable and with subtle colors, they appeal to the young as well as to those who like to feel comfortable in their shoes while remaining elegant.
There's a second store at Pasaz Myslbek; ☎ 224 232 234; Mon.-Fri. 9.30am-8pm, Sat. 9.30am-7pm, Sun. 10am-6pm.

HATS OF ALL SHAPES AND SIZES: A SPECIALTY OF PRAGUE

Hats are still being made in Prague, be it to protect oneself from the cold or the heat, or to wear for a special evening out. This long tradition has created women's hats, often with unusual shapes, made of felt or natural straw. A good address to seek out is:
Model Praha Družstvo
(Václavské nám. 28, ☎ 224 216 805;
Mon.-Fri. 9am-7pm, Sat. 10am-5pm).
This shop, nestling in a passageway, extends a very warm welcome and the helpful and friendly saleswomen know just how to make you feel at home before beginning the conversation about hats – custom-made, of course.

For the children

Prague is a wonderful place to buy traditional toys for children. Handcarved toys and wooden puppets will continue to delight children long after the latest electronic gadget has been tossed aside. It's an opportunity to fill up your Santa sack in readiness for Christmas!

Art Dekor

Ovocný trh 12
☎ 221 637 178
www.artdekor.cz
Mon.-Fri. 9.30am-7pm,
Sat.-Sun. 10am-6pm.

There are elephants with polka dots, rabbits with stripes, rhinos with flowers and many more unusual creatures. They are all handmade originals and prices range from Kč150 to Kč400. In this attractive store, you can buy a child's quilted bedspread to match the toy or choose a contrasting fun fabric to decorate their bedroom with on your return.

Obchods Loutkamy

Nerudova 47
☎ 257 532 735
Every day 10am-6pm.

This small shop sells very pretty, beautifully made wooden puppets, all of them made by Czech craftsmen. Numerous characters and animals inspired by fairy tales, everyday life or Czech television broadcasts sit quietly waiting for you next to delicate masks and beautiful decorative wooden birds.

Pecka – Modelář

Karoliny Světlé 3
☎ / 🏠 224 230 170
Zlatnická 4
☎ 222 323 445
Mon.-Fri. 9am-6pm,
Sat. 9am-noon.

Model enthusiasts will be excited to find rare Czech brands at excellent prices in this shop, which has two branches. You can buy a kit for the Škoda Favorit, the popular Czech car, costing Kč159 for the 96 rally version. If you'd prefer to make a model plane, they're also available here. Try to take advantage of the sales, when prices can be very attractive.

Classic Model

Bartolomějská 3
☎ 224 228 101
Mon.-Fri. 10am-6pm,
Sat. 9am-noon.

Lovers of electric trains will discover some little treasures among well-known brands (Roco) and Czech models (SVD, Bramos and MB). You'll also find clockwork metal models and other toys to add to your own system.

Sparkys

Havířská 2
☎ 224 239 309
Mon.-Sat. 10am-7pm,
Sun. 10am-6pm.

Fluffy toys, and yet more fluffy toys: this huge store, which spreads over four floors is, to the delight of old and young

alike, the paradise of stuffed toys. It is also a toy store where you can find nearly everything, from wooden toys to video games, not forgetting puzzles and books.

Galerie U Zrzavýho Kocoura

Palackého 11
☎ 224 94 73 81
Mon.-Fri. 10am-6pm,
Sat. 10am-3pm.

The brightly colored naive paintings on sale at Galerie U Zrzavýho Kocoura are very decorative, and some are already framed.

There are also drawings, reproductions and paintings on glass, ideal for hanging on children's bedroom walls. They come in a variety of subjects (from Noah's Ark to farm animals) and a wide range of prices (from Kč30 to Kč50,000!

Divadlo Minor

Vodičkova 6
☎ 222 23 17 02
www.minor.cz
Ticket office: ☎ 222 23 13 51

Since 1949, the Minor Theater has built its reputation on the quality of its clown and puppet shows. For children aged four and older, the performances, which last an hour, are scheduled in the daytime. The theater is located in the children's arcade (Dětská pasáž) where you will also find toy stores, children's clothes stores and a small café decorated with puppets.

Balet

Karolíny Světlé 22
☎ 222 22 10 63
Mon.-Wed. 10am-6pm,
Fri. 10am-5pm.

In this old shop, located close to the Vltava river, tutus hang from the ceiling and ballet shoes, pink tights and leotards galore await excited little ballet pupils. With its atmosphere steeped in classical dance, this shop is bound to impress children interested in ballet (prices from Kč500 to Kč7,000).

THE STORY OF MIKULÁŠ, A DEVIL AND AN ANGEL

On December 5, Mikuláš (St Nicholas) goes looking for children in the streets of Prague. Accompanied by a devil in red and an angel, he distributes treats to the well-behaved.
As night falls, the little citizens of Prague watch his carriage pass and hear the gifts being given out. Those who have misbehaved and are unable to recite a poem receive potatoes and coal instead of candy.

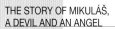

Musical
instruments and recordings

The Czech musical tradition goes back to the Middle Ages and the country has an excellent reputation for the quality of its musical instruments. Brass instruments made here are very reasonable. If you need to assemble an entire brass band, you'll be able to do it much more cheaply in Prague than in many other cities. Good secondhand bargains are around, but try not to fall under the spell of an antique Bohemian violin, which could seriously upset your finances.

Amati - Denak

U Obecního domu
☎ 222 00 23 46
Mon.-Fri. 10am-6pm,
Sat. 10am-1pm.

This store is next to the Municipal House and specializes in brass instruments from the Amati Kraslice workshops. Toward 1550, the first instrument makers set themselves up in the old mining town of Kraslice, a tradition which continued for more than 400 years. Clarinets, saxophones, trumpets, oboes, French horns and other instruments are sold here, including the *piccolo trumpet* (see also Ivan Berka Blues, p. 103)

Dům Hudebních nástrojů

Jungmannovo
náměstí 17
☎ 224 22 25 00
Mon.-Fri. 9am-6pm,
Sat. 9am-3pm.

Four floors entirely devoted to musical instruments: this store greatly deserves the name of "Guitar Park." In the basement, electric and acoustic guitars, including instruments by the Czech

manufacturer Rieger-Klass. On the first floor, there are wind instruments, on the second drums, electronic keyboards and various accessories and on the third floor, you'll find a collection of the beautiful Petrof pianos.

Ivan Berka Blues

Štěpánská 61,
Passage Lucerna
☎ 224 21 70 77
Mon.-Fri. 10am-7pm,
Sat. 10am-4pm.

The *piccolo trumpet* is made in the Czech Republic and is the smallest trumpet in the world. It looks at first just like a beautiful chrome toy, but once you hear some Baroque music being played on it, you realize it is far from being a mere plaything. You'll find them next to a range of acoustic and electric guitars,

not far from the saxophones, both new and secondhand.

Praha Music Center

Revoluční 14
☎ 222 311 693
Mon.-Fri. 9am-1pm, 2-6pm.

Praha Music Center brings together a great selection of copper instruments. If you've thought of initiating yourself into the difficult art of the sax then visit the specialists in this store who will be able to advise you. Between tubas and horns, the *piccolo trumpet* is Kč9,000.

Capriccio

Újezd 15
☎ 257 320 165
Mon.-Fri. 9am-6pm,
Sat. 10am-4pm.

Capriccio is a musical café: You come here to have a coffee,

and, if you feel like it, you can play something for the customers present (classical, jazz, country, pop music, etc. – everything is possible!). Specialized literature, scores and CDs are also for sale. The atmosphere is quite relaxed; musicians will enjoy it.

Hudební nástroje Radek Bubrle

Náprstkova 10
☎ 222 221 110
Mon.-Fri. 10am-6pm,
Sat. 10am-4pm.

You may be surprised to discover how much Czechs adore American country music, and it isn't just in response to the latest musical in town. It runs much deeper, as revealed by the cowboy jackets, saloon-style bars and Czech translations of song lyrics which you may encounter on your travels. In this store you can buy and sell secondhand and antique instruments on which to play your favorite folk and country music. You'll find a selection of concert programs next to the CDs.

U Zlatého Kohouta

Michalska 3
☎ 224 212 874
Mon.-Fri. 10am-6pm.

Old violins and cellos sit quietly in the window, but inside they are hanging nearly everywhere. You really feel as if you're entering a workshop rather than a store. This impression is reinforced by the sight of some instruments being repaired in the very middle of the shop. Sometimes a music lover will play right in front of you.

COMPLETE YOUR COLLECTION

Czech classical CDs are known for being well produced and less expensive than in other European countries – even if the choice is probably narrower than in your usual music store. So this is a great opportunity to build up your CD collection at a decent price. Here are three addresses which offer good selections:

Supraphon (classical): Jungmannova 20
☎ 224 94 87 19; Mon.-Fri. 9am-7pm, Sat. 9am-1pm.

Bontonland: Václavské nám. 1; ☎ 224 473 080
Mon.-Sat. 9am-8pm, Sun. 10am-7pm; in the basement, entrance via the Koruna Gallery.

Siroky Dvur: Loretanske nám. 4
☎ 220 515 403; Tue.-Sun. 10am-1pm and 2-6pm.

Jewelry
and crystal

Gems, precious stones, silver and pearls are all available in Prague. You can choose from genuine or costume jewelry, real or imitation, chic or kitsch. Don't forget to buy a set of crystal glasses to brighten up your table at home. They make an excellent conversation point.

Halada

Na příkopě 16
☎ 224 221 304
Mon.-Sat. 9am-7pm,
Sun. 10am-6pm.

This fashionable shop offers a wide selection of stylized jewelry with pure lines: earrings, bracelets, rings, pendants, and more. Made of gold, silver or pearls, set with precious stones or diamonds, they are often unique creations. As long as you are prepared to pay for them, this is a delightful way to get hitched. There's a second store at Parizska 7; ☎ 222 311 868; Mon.-Sat. 10am-7pm, Sun. 11am-7pm.

Nikkita & Inkognito

Opatovická 14
Mon.-Fri. 11am-7pm.

The colorful beads of the Inkognito collection of necklaces shimmer on their metal threads. There are also some attractive one-of-a-kind skirts and dresses bearing the successful Nikkita label. The entrance to the shop is in Novoměstská Passage.

East Art Gallery

Václavské náměstí 23
Every day 10am-8pm.

Great magical powers have been attributed to amber, and it is thought to be a fertility symbol and healing stone. Many jewelers in Prague work with yellow amber, which comes mostly from the Baltic region. However, be careful of the many imitations. You can check the quality by rubbing pieces of amber together and then sniffing them. You'll notice that it gives off a distinctive smell if it is the real thing. In this gallery you'll come across some fine amber pieces. Expect to pay

between Kč2,000 and Kč4,000 for a large necklace.

Material

U Luzického seminare 7
☎ 257 533 663
Every day 10.30am-8.30pm.

Not far from Charles Bridge, this small shop is the ideal place to find an unusual item with very delicate lines. Created in the Ajeto workshops by extremely inventive Czech designers, vases, glasses, candlesticks and chandeliers have shapes and colors you won't find anywhere else, except in the Arzenal gallery (see p. 58). Another advantage is that the prices are not prohibitive.

Belda

Mikulandská 10
☎ 224 93 30 52
Mon.-Fri. 10am-6pm.

The shop sign reminds us that this boutique has existed since 1922, but the Czech jewelry on display is unmistakably contemporary. A ring will cost Kč3,000 and a silver necklace with garnets Kč20,000. You can also find fantastic large-scale glass sculptures and the famous twisted plates of Czech designer Lhotský.

Granát Turnov

Dlouhá 28 and Panska 1
☎ 222 315 612
Mon.-Fri. 10am-6pm,
Sat. 10am-1pm.

This shop has a large selection of garnets, set in gold, silver and platinum, directly from a craftsmen's cooperative in Turnov. The pieces are original and sold at factory outlet prices. A silver or platinum garnet ring will cost from Kč1,500; Kč2,700 if set in gold.

Crystalex

Malé náměstí 6
☎ 224 22 84 59
Every day 10am-8pm.

Head for the Malá Strana along Melantrichova Street, where you'll pass several shops selling crystal. The windows are overflowing with glasses and decanters. At this Crystalex outlet you'll be able to buy a selection of pieces at modest prices. A set of six glasses will cost from Kč1,800. A decanter with a colored glass stopper will set you back around Kč455. The design of the pieces is mostly classic, cut, engraved and colored. If you need to buy a very special gift, then this is the place to come.

Miss Bijoux

Václavské nám. 23
☎ 224 213 627
Mon.-Sat. 10am-8pm,
Sun. 10am-6pm.

Looking at the fake crystal figurines, you might get the wrong impression. This shop also contains highly original works by young designers such as glass bead necklaces, earrings and brooches in colored glass paste. Other items include handpainted glass beads and many items of fantasy jewelry at reasonable prices.

TIPS ON TESTING THE QUALITY OF CRYSTAL

Bohemian glass is among the finest in the world. However, you should be aware that crystal can differ greatly depending on where it is made. You can recognize good-quality crystal by how smooth, solid and heavy it is. You'll also notice its rainbow-colored reflections and the perfection of its edges (in the case of cut glass). There should be no bubbles or faults, and if edges are rough and imperfect, the quality is probably mediocre. If a glass has not been cut by hand, you'll be able to feel and see a groove along the stem. A small bump on the base is another indicator. However, you should be aware that each handcut piece will be unique and may not be totally geometrical.

Stationery
and bookstores

In this hi-tech age of emails and the Internet, old-fashioned stationery still has a certain charm. If you still use pens and paper, you'll love looking around the stationery stores in Prague, where the products are amazing value. The notebooks and journals come in all shapes and sizes, from kitsch to art deco. Some stock is available on recycled paper, so you can be eco-friendly if you wish. Artists can also stock up on paper and materials here at very reasonable prices.

Tesco

Národní třída 26
☎ 222 00 31 11
Mon.-Fri. 8am-9pm,
Sat.-Sun. 9am-8pm.

Make sure you see the huge range of locally produced paper on the first floor.

There is also a traditional selection of notebooks and journals, some using recycled paper, plasticine, coloring books and pens of all shapes and sizes. Head for the giftwrap section, which is full of good ideas. You can decorate your gift with printed or gold paper, gift boxes and paper bows in all colors.

Papírnictví

Palackého 10
Mon.-Wed. 8.30am-6.30pm, Fri. 8.30am-6pm, Sat. 9am-noon.

If you are looking for a special atmosphere, this local stationery store is worth a little visit. Nestled at the back of a

mini-market, behind the food counters, it's an unusual compromise between a supermarket and a traditional store. Take a basket, ask the salesperson for advice to make your choice, then go to the till like everybody else.

Herliz

Dukelských hrdinů 39
Tram 12 and 7, stop: Štrossmayerovo nám.
☎ 233 38 00 02
Mon.-Fri. 8.30am-6pm,
Sat. 9am-noon.

The way this shop works is self-service: You take a (compulsory) basket and help yourself. As a result, you can take as long as you like and stroll through the aisles. You can find the same items as in Tesco but a little cheaper.

Family Museum of Postcards

Liliová 4
☎ 222 222 519
Tue.-Sun. 11am-7pm.

This museum is a real treasure trove if you want to stock up on old-fashioned Czech postcards: greeting cards, birthday cards, Christmas cards and even "declaration of love" cards, the boater-and-lace-petticoat kind. They are reproductions of the 1,200 old cards filling up the display shelves of this museum where furniture of the 1950s also features prominently. The cards are reasonable (Kč12). Books about Prague postcards are also for sale.

Decorative Arts Museum shop

17 Listopadu 2
☎ 251 093 265
Tue.-Sun. 10am-6pm.

In this tiny shop, tucked away under the steps leading to the museum itself, you'll come across notebooks and good-quality exercise books with art-nouveau patterns, books about architecture and the Biedermeier style (1815–48), albums with reproductions of old postcards of the Jewish district, brooches, and more. To regain your strength, you can sit down in the museum café in front of the showcases full of old clocks.

Knihkupectvi Kanzelsberger

Václavské náměstí 4
☎ 224 219 214
Every day 9am-8pm.

On five floors, this huge bookstore lets you choose a book, a score or a postcard – this is not an exhaustive list – and also relax in a comfortable café, a sophisticated setting with moldings, gildings and a beautiful fireplace, where the works of Czech artists are displayed. The books in foreign languages (translations of works by famous Czech authors, art books, dictionaries and language teaching courses) are displayed on the top floor.

Kafkovo Knihkupectvi

Staroměstské náměstí 12
☎ 222 321 454
Every day 10am-7pm.

If you want to take the opportunity of staying in Prague to discover or read again the great Czech authors, you should stop in this small bookstore set up in the

splendid Kinský Palace. From Kafka to Kundera via Václav Havel and Jaroslav Hašek, your only difficulty will be making a choice. You'll also find art and architecture books in English and a wide selection of postcards.

Zlatá Loď'

Národní 37
Passage Platýz
☎ 222 220 174
Mon.-Fri. 9am-7pm,
Sat. 10am-5pm.

This is a good place to buy art materials at extremely reasonable prices. It also offers an excellent opportunity to test out some locally made products (from Kč344 to Kč593 for 48 pastels, from Kč852 to Kč2,457 for a wooden box containing 24 watercolors).

Altamira

Jilská 2
☎ 224 21 99 50
Mon.-Fri. 9am-7pm,
Sat. 10am-5pm.

You can hardly put one foot in front of the other in this shop. The items are piled on top of one another apparently at random. Customers are not allowed to touch anything and have to wait to be served. You'll find all the basic artist's materials for oil painting, water colors, modeling and sculpture for sale here, so come and stock up.

ALL THE COLORS OF THE RAINBOW

Koh-i-Noor has nothing to do with the famous diamond, but it's certainly a gem of a brand. It has an excellent range of pencils at good prices, made in České Budějovice. Individual lead pencils cost Kč3, a wooden box of ten costs Kč127, and you'll pay from Kč135 for colored pencils. Children will love the large container in the shape of a colored pencil full of crayons (Kč29 for 12 and Kč427 for the full container). The brand is available in most stationery stores in Prague.

Shopping malls
and markets

Faded arcades and dark passages with empty shopwindows are things of the past. Although the splendid Lucerna Palace (see p. 61) is still awaiting a restoration worthy of its reputation, the shopping malls with their modern architecture are every bit a match for those of the other European capital cities. As for the markets, they are full of goods of every kind, cheerfully, if chaotically, displayed. They offer a more practical and often cheaper alternative to the mainstream stores.

Shopping malls

Cerna Ruze

Na příkopě 12
Every day 7am-9pm;
stores: Mon.-Fri. 10am-8pm,
Sat. 10am-7pm, 11am-7pm.

Sober and elegant, this shopping mall stretches over three floors and proves to be rather cozy, away from the hustle and bustle prevailing outside. Here you can find numerous chic or sportswear fashion shops, including one belonging to the designer Jozef Sloboda (see p. 96), toy stores, delicatessens, as well as a restaurant, a bar and a café where you can sit outside.

Pasaz Mylsbek

Na příkopě 19/21
Mon.-Sat. 8.30am-8.30pm,
Sun. 9.30am-8.30pm.

Opened in October 1996, this *pasaz* with an ultramodern

design is the joint work of Czech architects Zdenek Hölzel and Jan Kerel, and of Frenchman Claude Parent. Set in a refined decor of marble and granite, this mall in the very heart of Prague, which links the modern Na příkopě to the ancient Ovocný trh, spreads over two floors and houses about 30 stores and two restaurants.

Metropole Zlicin

Revnicka 5
Metro Zlicin
Every day 10am-9pm.

This huge shopping center is not located in the city center,

fruits, almonds, chocolate-covered nuts and dried bananas in locally made yoghurt (about Kč25 per 100g/3.5oz). It's a good place to stock up on nourishing food on a chilly day.

but at the exit of the Zlicin station (B line). However, it is only about 20 minutes by subway from Můstek station. Ultramodern and bright, it is arranged over two levels around a fountain and very modern footbridges. Restaurants and cafés are upstairs, along a mezzanine which overlooks the first floor shops. Most of the well-known Czech companies have opened shops here and, the cherry on the cake, a huge Electro World is devoted to image, sound and video games.

Local markets

Havelský trh. (Havel market)

Havelská
Mon.-Fri. 8am-6pm,
Sat. 9am-1pm.

In this open-air market, with its huge selection of vegetables, cut flowers and pots of honey, you'll find craft items, such as painted eggs (Kč150-300), postcards and prints. There is a friendly, relaxed atmosphere, so take time to wander around and hunt out little wooden gifts or pendants set with stones (from Kč50).

Správa Tržiště

Near Národní třída metro
Mon.-Fri. 9am-5pm,
Sat.-Sun. 9am-4pm.

Outside Tesco there is a fruit and vegetable market. The produce is good value but the quality can vary, depending on the season. You can buy dried

Seasonal markets

At Christmas and Easter, market stands are set up on the Old Town Square and at the lower end of Wenceslas Square. The locals come to keep warm with a glass of mulled wine, while tourists walk around the stalls, tempted by the smell of grilled sausages with bread and mustard (*párek*). Painted eggs, beeswax candles and straw decorations are on sale at Christmas, along with other crafts. It's quite a festive event.

THE NEW SHOPPING MALLS OF PRAGUE

With the steady commercialization of Prague has come a new lease on life for the malls (*pasaz*). The luxury shops of former years have been replaced by big foreign labels and local companies. Don't miss the two most beautiful art-nouveau malls, which have been recently restored. The Koruna Palace (1910–14) is at Wenceslas Square, while the Adria Palace (1923–25) is at Národní třída, 40. As you do your window-shopping, take time to admire the beautiful surroundings, with all the chrome, mirrors, marble and glass domes. Both malls look very impressive at night when they are lit up – try and visit them if you have time.

Local crafts

Wooden objects, puppets, crystal and traditional blue tablecloths are probably the most common examples of Czech crafts, but you'll also find there is a wide range of good-quality, reasonably priced small gifts to take home. If you come to the city in December, you can also look for Christmas decorations – which will add a hint of Bohemia to your usual festive decor.

Linke
Narodni trida 37, pasaz Platyz
☎ 224 213 274
Mon.-Fri. 10am-6pm.
Mikulandksa 2
☎ 224 933 057.

Both addresses are real gold mines if you wish to give a new look to your home for a reasonable price. Besides a wide choice of Czech-made materials, plain or patterned and sold by the meter, you'll find many cushions, pillows and duvets in pleasant colors. The very young are not forgotten either because lots of items are designed especially for them and to decorate their cribs.

Romen Shop
Nerudova 32
Tue.-Sun. 10am-6pm.

Having a passion for the Romany culture, Petra, Pavlina and Richard travel up and down the Czech Republic for several months a year to collect items made by the *tziganes*. As a result, their shop has the appearance of an art gallery – with paintings, photographs, children's drawings, clothes, jewelry, calendars, CDs and more. More than 50 percent of the sales are passed on to the Romany creators.

Keramika
U Luzického seminare 8
☎ 603 461 470
Every day 11am-7pm.

Not far from Charles Bridge, this pretty little shop offers a large choice of pottery made by various craftspeople from different workshops in the region. This explains why the styles can be very different

and why certain pieces are unique. Bowls, vases, cups— you can find a little of everything, especially items in a magnificent shade of blue and glazed porcelain tablewear.

Móda Original

Jungmannova 13
☎ 296 245 033
Mon.-Fri. 10am-6pm.

From the blue ceramics with their stylized motifs, beeswax candles and stationery to the tablecloths, place mats and linen dresses and blouses, everything in this shop is handmade in the Czech Republic. With their simple lines and subtle colors (China blue and soft green), the clothes are both elegant and attractive.

Sejto

Doulhá 24
☎ 222 320 370
Mon.-Fri. 10am-7pm,
Sat. 11am-5pm.
Alternative store at no. 21 on the Castle's Golden Lane.

Since 1995, Alexandra Dýckova and Jarmila Dunděrova have drawn their inspiration from ancient Bohemian crafts to create a refined and warm atmosphere around their fabrics. The subtle harmonies of colors are reminiscent of Chinese fabrics. Linen place mats, cotton tablecloths, silk cushions, printed natural material – the result is enchanting. Unmissable.

Kavka Workshop

Elišky Krasnohorské 3
☎ 224 828 249
Mon.-Fri. 10am-6pm.

If you love antique furniture but don't like restoring it, then this is the place for you. This is a shop brimming with old wooden Czech furniture, cleaned, renovated and waxed. There is a huge selection of items, all ready to go, including chests of drawers, wardrobes, dressers, chairs and tables. The prices are attractive, too, between around Kč3,000 to Kč15,000. They will be happy

to give you information about transporting goods home.

Keramika

Havelska 21
☎ 224 219 210
and 224 214 176
Mon.-Fri. 10am-7pm,
Sat.-Sun. 10am-6pm.

These typically Czech pottery items are exclusively crafted in Tupesy in Southern Moravia. Traditionally decorated in blue and white, they can also be extremely colorful. This tiny shop offers a wide selection where, when it comes to taste, you can find the best and the worst. Dishes, plates, egg-cups, jars of different sizes and even surprising small pottery figures make memorable souvenirs.

Bytový Textil

Masná 20
☎ 224 817 059
Mon.-Fri. 10am-6pm.

Cushions, household linen, tablecloths, curtains, bedspreads, embroidery, canvas and colored materials (plain or patterned) sold by the meter; you are very likely to find what you are looking for in this well-ordered and welcoming little shop. You'll also find delightful cloth animals to keep the children happy.

CESKÁ LIDOVÁ REMESLA

You'll recognize this chain from the shopwindows, which are always full to the brim with wooden objects and blue printed fabrics. All the natural products give the stores a warm and inviting atmosphere. You can buy embroidered tablecloths (Kč1,635), wicker baskets (Kč375), painted eggs (Kč50-180), virgin wool sweaters (Kč4,500), kitchen equipment (Kč15-90) and small decorative items. You should visit one of their eight stores to see the best of traditional Czech crafts.
Try the store at:
Melantrichova, 17
Mon.-Fri. 10am-7pm, Sat.-Sun. 10am-7.30pm.

Sports

Although the Czechs have produced such wonderful tennis players as Jana Novotná, Petr Korda, Ivan Lendl and the great Martina Návratilová, the national sport is ice hockey, and children can be seen skating on the smallest pond in winter. The Czechs are extremely proud of their national team, which beat the USSR in August 1968, Canada in 1996 and became Olympic champions at Nagano in 1998. More than 100,000 people gathered in the Old Town Square to give the players a hero's welcome on their return from Japan. It was a triumph for Jaromír Jáger and Dominik Hašek, the two most popular players in the team.

JB Sport

Dlážděná 3
☎ 224 210 921
🖷 224 210 951
Mon.-Fri. 9am-6pm,
Sat. 9am-1pm.
There are two sports stores in

the same street, one of which sells only ice hockey equipment. You'll find every accessory imaginable, from sticks to skates, not to mention the inevitable national team shirts – every supporter of the modern-day Czech heroes should have one.

Hudy Sport

Slezská 8
☎ 222 52 24 50
Mon.-Fri. 9am-6.30pm,
Sat. 9am-1pm.
Na Perstyne 14
☎ 224 218 600
Mon.-Fri. 9am-6.30pm,
Sat. 10am-2pm.

A very good store to get a new pair of walking shoes, rainproof

gear or mountain wear, sleeping bags, backpacks and all your essential outdoor sports equipment. They even have a small climbing area and a collection of regional maps in the basement.

Mystic Skates

Stepanská 31
☎ 222 232 027
Mon.-Fri. 10am-7pm,
Sat. 10am-3pm.

Lovers of skateboards and
snowboards, on your mark,
get set, go! There are boards
absolutely everywhere, not to
mention matching caps, shoes
and outfits.

SportTown

Václavské náměstí 22
☎ 234 097 070
Every day 10am-8pm.

Every label and every sport has
a place of honor in this huge
store devoted only to sports
and displaying posters of
famous sportsmen. On three
floors you'll find on display
items from all the international
brands.

Dušan Wiegler – Humi

Martinská 2,
☎ 224 22 50 85
Mon.-Wed. 9am-6.30pm, Wed.-
Fri. 9am-7pm, Sat. 10am-1pm.

This small shop sells everything
you need to go trekking, from
sleeping bags to tent pegs.
There is even an indoor
climbing wall. The staff is
friendly and informative, and
will advise you on the best
places to go trekking in the
Czech Republic.

Kiwi

Jungmannova 23
☎ 224 94 84 55
🖷 296 24 55 55
Mon.-Fri. 9am-7pm,
Sat. 9am-2pm.

This is a great find for those
interested in walking or
mountain biking. You'll find the
usual travel guides in different
languages, touring and city
maps, and more unusual and
interesting maps on footpaths
in the Czech Republic,
France and Spain that are very
reasonably priced. You might
even be lucky enough to come
across a map of the Battle of
Normandy, if you're interested
in historical detail.

Giga Sport

Na příkopě 19/21,
pasaz Mylsbek
☎ 224 237 494
Every day 9.30am-7.30pm.

Whatever sport you participate
in, here you'll find the
equipment and outfit you're
looking for. The choice is
amazing and the prices
reasonable.

Association Club Sparta Praha

Milady Horákové 98
Prague 120 00
☎ 222 220 424
Mon.-Fri. 10am-5pm.

Sparta Prague is the Czech
Republic's best soccer team.
It has more titles than any other
Czech club and its stadium in
Letná has the most modern
equipment. Fans come to
matches in droves and shop
here for their tickets, flags,
scarves and shirts. It's a
treasure trove of soccer
paraphernalia.

DANA AND EMIL ZÁTOPEK

Dana and Emil Zátopek were both born in 1922 and achieved
great success together 30 years later at the Olympic Games in
Helsinki in 1952. Emil Zátopek became the only athlete in
sporting history to be triple champion in the 5,000- and
10,000-meter events, plus the marathon. On the day of his first
win, his wife, Dana, took the gold medal for the javelin throw.
The holder of nine world records, Emil Zátopek, who died in
November 2000, is still revered by his country for his sporting
achievements.

Antiques
and bric-a-brac

When you go looking for antiques, you'll have the choice of luxurious shops or more humble market stands. There are some good bargains to be had, from the smallest trinket to a magnificent silver service, so spend time taking a good look around and you're likely to be well rewarded. The professionals are probably a few steps ahead of you, but there's a wide choice for all tastes and budgets.

Alma

Valentinská 7
☎ 222 325 865
et 224 813 991
Every day 10am-6pm.

On the first floor of a somewhat faded art-nouveau building, two fine shops display a wide range of often very interesting things. The one located at the corner of the Valentinská and Veleslavinova streets, elegant and with a quiet atmosphere, offers furniture, lamps, paintings, tableware, glasses and silverware. In the other one, smaller and more cozy,

don't forget to go downstrairs to the basement level where

you will discover fine laces, old fountain pens, hatpins and jewels from the 1920s and 1930s.

Bric-a-Brac

Týnská 7
☎ 222 326 484
Every day 11am-7pm.

This is a good example of a Prague bazaar. Located just behind the Týn church, it has a large selection of more unusual stock at a variety of prices. You'll find old jewelry, lamps, watches, pens, typewriters and cameras mixed up with posters and other old advertising material. Beware the prices – the shop is in the heart of the tourist area.

Dorotheum

Ovocný trh 2
☎ 224 222 001
www.dorotheum.cz
Mon.-Fri. 10am-6pm,
Sat. 10am-5pm.
Opened in 1992 (and at this address since 1998), this

branch of the famous Viennese company founded in 1707 contains real treasures: paintings, glasses, crystal, china, silverware, jewelry and ornamental items. Maybe you'll be lucky and find a superb silver teapot or an art-nouveau vase in glass paste. In this luxurious store items

presented at auction sales are on display for the public.

Galerie Ztichla Klika

Betlémská 10-14
☎ 222 222 079
et 222 221 561
Mon.-Fri. 10am-6pm.

Located at no. 10, Jan Placak's small bookstore is a real gold mine of secondhand books in Czech and German, but also sometimes in English or French. Some years ago it was extended with a gallery which regularly stages exhibitions, and with an antique

shop, both of them specializing in collectors' editions. Apart from more or less antique books (mainly in Czech, German or Latin), some of them decorated with beautiful ex libris, you can find a very interesting choice of engravings, posters, cards and photographs.

Az Manesova – Antik Galerie Bazar

Manesova 73
☎ 222 724 982
Mon.-Fri. 10am-6pm.

In a quiet pretty street lined with fashionable buildings on either side, this basement shop offers a large selection of charming objects for those who like to hunt for antiques. Here you can find absolutely everything: paintings, engravings, furniture, lamps, tableware, glasses, sewing machines or typewriters, stuffed animals, and even a raccoon! And who knows, maybe you'll discover a rare item!

Jan Pazdera

Vodičkova 28
☎ 224 216 197
Mon.-Fri. 10am-6pm,
Sat. 10am-1pm.

This is the place to come if you are an amateur photographer. Located at the start of the U Nováku arcade on Vodičkova Street, this shop is difficult to

miss. It has all the latest cameras alongside old models that have seen lots of action. You may have to wait a little while to be served but it is certainly worth it.

Starožitné Hodiny

Mikulandská 10
☎ 224 930 172
Mon.-Fri. 9am-noon
and 2pm-6pm.

Travel back in time at this antique shop, which specializes in antique watches, clocks and old alarm clocks. You won't beat any records on prices (a chronometer costs around Kč350, for example), but make sure you look at the superb Omega watches (from Kč1,200 to Kč4,000) and the fob watches (from Kč900 to Kč4,000). Take time out here.

Antik Mucha

Liliová 12
☎ 222 221 523
Mon.-Sat. 10am-6pm.

Petr and Miroslav, the partners who run this workshop, two minutes' walk from Charles Bridge, understand what the tourists are looking for: items that are transportable, valuable but not too expensive. Their den is crammed with closets full of china and art-nouveau decorative objects. There are also antique dolls and icons.

Nové schody zámecké.

Secondhand
books

Secondhand books are often sold in upscale stores, and as much attention and shelf space is given to them as to new publications. Almost all booksellers have foreign-language books (English-language bookstores are known as *knihkupectví* and are supported by the expatriate community). It's also worth searching for old maps, atlases, prints and postcards, many of which can be fascinating. You won't be able to go far without coming across a secondhand bookseller.

Antikvariát
Valentinská 8
☎ 224 816 253
Mon.-Fri. 10am-6pm,
Sat. 10am-2pm.

Here you can find secondhand books in Czech, German or English. You can also discover beautiful pictures at reasonable prices, art books in many language and a fine collection of classical music LP records.

Antikvariát
U Karlova mostu
Karlova 2
☎ 222 22 02 86
Mon.-Fri. 10am-6pm,
Sat. 11am-4pm.

A stone's throw from Charles Bridge is an absolute haven for lovers of rare books, old world maps and old prints.

There are also foreign language books to hunt through. If you feel like spending an hour or so in a bookstore, then this is a good place to choose.

Antikvariát Galerie
Můstek
Národní třída 40,
palác Adria
☎ 224 94 95 87
Mon.-Fri. 10am-6pm, Sat. noon-4pm, Sun. 2pm-6pm.
Even though this secondhand bookstore does stock some English books, it mostly sells German- and Czech-language publications. All the same, it is well worth a visit if

only to admire its beautiful collection of posters, engravings and old postcards. Given the quality of the works, it will not come as a surprise that they are not particularly cheap. The entrance is in the Adria Palace passage.

U Zlaté Číše

Nerudova 16
☎ 257 531 393
Every day 10am-6pm.

Among the timeless collections of postcards, engravings, old movie magazines and literary works in Czech and German, you'll find a selection of fine art books, and several shelves devoted to inexpensive books. They even have a few old kitsch photographs.

Antikvariát Ptolomaeus

Široká 15
☎ 222 329 985
Every day 10.30am-6pm.

Named in honor of Ptolemy, the famous second-century Greek geographer and astronomer, this shop offers a vast choice of maps, both earthly and heavenly. They are absolutely everywhere and you won't fail to discover some very unusual ones. You'll also find some beautiful old books, pictures and watercolors.

Antikvariát

Myslíkova 10 – Prague 2
☎ 224 917 862
Mon.-Fri. 9am-6pm,
Sat. 10am-2pm.

A study published in 2005 confirmed that the Czechs spend more time reading than any other nation. Just walking up and down the well-stocked set of shelves of this bookstore will convince you of this. This is a booklover's paradise. If you're looking for bargains, you may find cheap botanical plates, engravings and old books of photographs by Karel Plicka or Jindřich Eckert.

Antikvariát

Široká 7
☎ 222 318 876
Mon.-Fri. 10am-6pm,
Sun. 10am-4pm.

A pleasant scent of pipe tobacco greets you as you enter this shop, which is close to the Jewish quarter. There are many works of literature in German, English and even Hebrew. On the walls numerous pictures, lithographs, etchings and old photographs. Have a good browse.

Antikvariát

Vinohradska 66
☎ 224 251 220
Mon.-Fri. 10am-7pm,
Sat. 10am-noon.

If books written in Czech don't appeal to you, take a look at the art books for which knowledge of the language is not always a prerequisite. Music lovers can rummage among secondhand records, CDs and cassettes, and even be tempted by old original scores. If you'd like to discover *Carmen* in German, it is the ideal opportunity!

IN CUBIST SURROUNDINGS

This bookstore is located on the first floor and basement of the first cubist house built anywhere in the world. See p. 55 for more information on the "House of the Black Virgin" (1911–12). You can buy beautiful art books, exhibition catalogs and works on the history of the Czech Republic, all at very competitive prices compared to other outlets.

Knihkupectví U Černé Matky boží, Celetná 34
☎ 224 222 349
Mon.-Fri. 9.30am-7pm, Sat. 10am-7pm, Sun. 10am-6pm.

Design
and decoration

There's really no limit to what you can buy in Prague, however out of the ordinary. For example, you'll have no difficulty finding fancy dress clothes, especially if you're in need of a cowboy outfit. You can buy magic potions, eco-friendly lotions and even a suit of armor. We've selected a few of the more interesting and unusual stores for you.

Modernista

Konvitská 5
☎ 222 22 01 13
et 602 305 633
www.modernista.cz
Mon.-Fri. 2pm-6pm,
Sat. 11am-4pm and by
appointment.

For the fans of Czech cubism, functionalism, Bauhaus and industrial art deco. Desks, armchairs, lamps, tea and coffee services, small boxes, clocks: You will find originals here, lovingly restored, and limited edition copies, scrupulously put together using ancient materials and techniques, in collaboration

with the Prague Decorative Arts Museum. Well worth seeing,

if only to discover the extraordinary vitality of Czech modernism between the wars.

Qubus Design Studio

Ramová 3
☎ 222 313 151
Mon.-Fri. 10am-6pm,
Sat. 11am-4pm

You step into this tiny shop as into a house, up some steps flanked by wooden shutters. Young Czech designers offer their latest creations, fashioned using mainly plastic and ceramic. Side by side with numerous objects and gadgets which will easily find a place in your home, you'll discover some jewelry and photographs.

Art Decoratif

Michalská 19
☎ 225 777 156
Mon.-Sun. 10am-8pm.

If you are a lover of art nouveau, the whole universe of this artistic movement, so creative and original in Prague,

is gathered in this unmissable shop. The objects, all of them worthy of interest, are generally copies of originals, such as the reproductions of works by Mucha or Gallé. Lamps, glasses and decanters are quietly waiting for you to fall in love with them. Especially worth mentioning is the very beautiful jewelry, also copies of originals.

Botanicus

Týnský dvůr čp. 3
☎ 224 89 54 46
Every day 10am-8pm.

This shop is located in the beautiful Týn courtyard. Everything is natural and made following traditional methods as practised in Ostra, a "green" village north of Prague. Great attention is paid to the packaging of the

products, which turns a small purchase into a lovely gift. Choose from eucalyptus soap, round canisters of tea and pretty bottles of flavored vinegar, including such unusual varieties as orange and cardamom.

Plakatovani

Rybná 21
☎ 224 819 359
www.plakatovani.cz
Mon.-Fri. 9am-6pm.

A gold mine if you are looking for original 1920s and 1930s movie posters and copies of old advertising prints, or if you are interested in the propaganda of the communist age ("drinking is anti-communist, and encourages the return of capitalism," 1952). The shop has some originals (which cost between Kč1,000 and Kč9,500) but also stocks excellent copies (costing between Kč80 and Kč120). Also for sale are imitations of 19th-century paintings representing Bohemian castles.

Galerie U Rytíře Kryštofa

Kozňa 8
☎ 224 23 63 00
Every day 11am-8pm.

The medieval theme is very popular in Prague, and can be seen at most village festivals and fairs. On these occasions, tents are erected in the streets, and there are dances, sword fights, huge vats of soup and plenty of mead. In this shop you'll find armor, swords and sabers for enthusiasts, together with copies of models exhibited in Golden Lane (see p. 38). Wander around the shop to the melodious sound of medieval music, and you'll be transported back in time.

Secondhand

In Prague, secondhand clothes stores have traditionally sold to senior citizens who couldn't afford anything else – hence the limited assortment in most stores. But the trend is changing and young people are now opening their own stores with new exciting ideas. On the other hand, secondhand CDs are on sale everywhere, and you may possibly come across a few collector's items. It's certainly worth taking a good look around.

Toalette

Karolíný Světlé 9
☎ 224 234 729
Mon.-Wed. 10am-7pm,
Fri. 10am-6pm.

Here is a particularly original boutique, whose style is difficult to define. A colorful mixture of 1940s polka dot fabrics and the most eccentric 1970s accessories. They sell everything from jackets, pants, skirts, scarves and handkerchiefs to necklaces and purses.

Second-Hand-Markt

Jungmannova 16
Prague 1
Mon.-Fri. 9.30am-6.30pm,
Sat. 9.30am-12.30pm.

You'll find a jumble of second-hand clothes in this store which occupies two levels. Not only jackets, skirts, dresses and shirts, but also bathrobes and swimsuits and a large quantity of scarves (Kč30) are on sale. You pay at the cash desk in the entrance either by item (Kč30-500) or by weight, according to the type of clothes.

Antique Military Shop

Pasáž Metro / Národní 25
☎ 224 238 285
Mon.-Fri. 10am-7pm,
Sat. 11am-5pm, Sun. 1-6pm.

To protest against the war in Iraq, several young Czechs have set themselves alight, as Jan Palach did in protest against the Russian invasion in 1969. In this shop selling military relics, it is common to buy secondhand combat uniforms to wear in anti-war protest marches. You can also find officer uniforms and Russian *kepis* (peaked caps) left by the occupying forces, along with leather items displaying the hammer and sickle.

CD Bazar

Jungmannova 13
☎ 604 928 143
Mon.-Fri. 10am-7pm.

You can't miss this shop.
Just follow the arrows into
the courtyard and to the
end of the passage – or let
yourself be guided by the
music. The tiny shop is at the
end. It stocks movie DVDs
and a small selection of CDs.
You pay cash with a 50
percent discount.

Bazar CD

Jindrisska 17
☎ 222 240 914
Mon.-Fri. 9am-7pm,
Sat. 10am-2pm.

Masses of CDs, DVDs and
videocassettes. This is not
a secondhand store, but
the prices are often very
inexpensive. As for the music,
the choice is impressive: Czech
light music, classical music,
but mainly jazz, rock, pop,
hip-hop and rap.

Vintage

Michalská 18
☎ 777 273 238
Mon.-Fri. 10am-8pm,
Sat. 11am-6pm, Sun. 1pm-5pm.

A native of St Petersburg,
Natalia is in her 30s and
has two secondhand shops
in the center of Prague.

The young love them.
Natalia travels to Italy, the
Netherlands and Great Britain
and, in her heavy trunks,
she brings back oddments
and secondhand clothes,
handmade garments of the
1960s. The shop is festive and
colorful: belts, hats, purses,
caps and ties (a little too
kitsch!). There are also some
fine examples of diamanté
dresses. Natalia's other shop
is Retro (Uhelný trh 9,
☎ 224 215 351, same
opening hours).

CD Bazar Gung-Ho

Rock Café
Národní 20
☎ 224 919 103
Mon. 10am-5pm, Tue. 2pm-
9pm, Wed. 2pm-7pm, Fri.
10am-5pm.

Only visit the Rock Café Club
downstairs if you're a fan of

hard rock, trash metal or heavy
metal – anyone else will be
disappointed. There are
T-shirts, videocassettes and
even vinyl records on sale.

Bazar CD LP

Krakovska 4
☎ 602 313 730
Mon.-Fri. 9am-7pm,
Sat. 10am-1pm.

Nearly all the items are
secondhand in this store. It
offers a wide choice of CDs
and vinyl records, but also
audio- and videocassettes,
DVDs and posters. Sometimes
you can discover real little
treasures. So if you're
looking for a particular CD
or a collection vinyl record this
is the place to come. It is the
largest store of its kind in the
Czech Republic, with 20,000
titles available.

BS FOTO

If there is always a crowd of tourists (men and women)
congregating in front of Jiří Linger's small lab, they are there
to cast an inquisitive glance at a row of old and somewhat
risqué stereoscopic photographs, propped up against the
shopwindow. Other curiosities inside are Kodak cameras more
than 100 years old, Leicas from the 1940s, the famous 9mm
Siemens movie cameras, Birnbaum bellows cameras, opera
glasses and even a pocket camera once used by the KGB.

Betlémské náměstí 7
☎ 222 221 605
Mon.-Fri. 10am-6pm.

Gourmet
specialties

The most renowned and enjoyed liquid specialty in Prague is beer. However, there are some other gastronomic surprises in store for you, too, including sausages and salamis, cheeses and sweet pastries. You should also sample at least one of the fruit brandies for which Bohemia and Moravia are famous, including, of course, the renowned *slivovice*.

Cellarius

Lucerna
Štěpánská 61
☎ 224 21 09 79
Mon.-Sat. 10.30am-9pm,
Sun. 10.30am-8pm.

As your eye travels along the wooden shelves in this shop

you'll see local liqueurs, wine and other types of alcohol rubbing shoulders with bottles from all over the world. The Czech fruit brandies made by Jelínek are recognizable by their pretty hexagonal bottles. A bottle of Bohemian kirsch or apricot-based Meruňkovice will cost around Kč350.

Lahůdky Zlatý Kříž

Jungmannova 19
☎ 221 191 801
Mon.-Fri. 6.30am-7pm,
Sat. 9am-3pm.

Becherovka is a bittersweet, yellow herbal drink, which can be served as an aperitif, a liqueur or as a cocktail with the local Beton tonic.

It comes in a green bottle with a yellow label and is made from herbs soaked in the curative thermal waters of the town of Karlovy Vary. It is reputed to help digestion, because of the powers of the water. There is only one way to find out if it works for you!

Lahůdky Zemark

Václavské náměstí 42
☎ 224 217 326
Mon.-Fri. 7am-7.30pm,
Sat. 10am-6pm.

The district is undergoing a complete transformation, but this traditional grocery store is resisting valiantly. Fully renovated, it offers a range of tasty cheeses and cold meats

as Czech as the customers. Why not treat yourself to a *chlebíčky*, which you can eat standing at a table? You can also find a wide choice of spirits, wines and liqueurs here, especially the famous *slivovice* plum brandy (45°), a Moravian specialty. One of the best brands is Jelínek, packaged in round bottles (0.75 liter) or in slim, tall bottles (0.5 liter).

Včelařská prodejna bistro

Křemencova 8
☎ 224 934 344
Mon.-Wed. 9am-5pm,
Tue. 9am-6pm, Wed. 9am-7pm,
Fri. 9am-2pm.

Prague's honey specialist, this shop sells everything to do with honey, from professional beekeeping equipment (hives, protection suits, masks, etc.) to honey-based liqueurs and wines, nectar, royal jelly and a large variety of locally produced honeys and beauty products. Honey lovers in Prague should absolutely taste *perník*, a local specialty similar to gingerbread, which you can buy in most bakeries.

Vinné Bistro Vivo

Maltezské náměstí 3
☎ 257 531 472
Mon.-Fri. 11am-9pm,
Sat. 2pm-9pm.

The Czech Republic produces very good wines, especially the Moravian province, and this shop is a good place to discover them. The wines are displayed on the first floor and the sampling, free of charge, takes place in the cellar (Tue.-Fri. from 3pm). The welcome is warm and the advice excellent. You can also find teas and coffees, and enjoy a freshly ground coffee at the bar.

Cukrárna Simona

Václavské náměstí 14
☎ 224 22 75 35
Mon.-Fri. 9am-8pm, Sat.
10am-8pm, Sun. 10am-8pm.

This small confectioner's shop sells Czech spirits and liqueurs, a selection of chocolates and the famous pancakes from Karlovy Vary, the *Oplatky Kolonáda*. They are available in a variety of flavors, including nut and chocolate. You can buy them in canisters or from the street vendors in the main tourist areas, who serve them hot.

Prodejna U Salvátora

Náprstkova 2
☎ 222 22 11 61
Mon.-Fri. 10am-6pm.

This little spice shop is located not far from the Vltava river, and is reached down a little cobblestone alleyway. As soon as you open the door you're greeted by a wonderful smell of spices – basil, thyme, vanilla, aniseed and cinnamon. On one side there's a menu showing all the herbs and spices, with at least ten different types of pepper (Kč35 per 30g/1oz for the green variety). On the other side are descriptions of all the prepared mixtures (e.g. *gulasové* for goulash, Kč12), which are sold in small packets at low prices.

ABSINTHE, 70 PERCENT ALCOHOL!

The Czech Republic is one of the few countries where absinthe is still a popular drink. Van Gogh's favorite tipple is a very powerful substance, made from fermented wormwood and banned in most Western countries at some stage, accused of causing seizures and hallucinations in heavy drinkers. A viscous green liquid, absinthe won't be served today with an absinthe spoon to pour sugar through the holes as it was at the beginning of the last century. Nowadays it is usually served neat without ice. To help this emerald green, plant-based drink which is 70° proof go down, don't hesitate to mix it with water and sugar (it still remains very strong).

Practicalities

What time do people go out?

A night out in Prague starts quite early. The locals head for the restaurants at 7pm, which is also the time the curtain goes up at the opera. Jazz clubs warm up at around 9pm, but nightclubs don't really get going until 11pm and close their doors between 3 and 5am. You should note that events start on time in Prague, and doors close promptly. Be punctual when going to the opera, theater or a concert, or you may find you're not allowed in. On the whole you'll find that the nightlife is relatively inexpensive.

Finding out what's on

There are three booklets in English to find out everything happening in town: *In your pocket*, *Events in Prague* and *Prague, this month* on sale at newspaper kiosks. To find out all the programs, consult the website of the Ticketpro and Bohemia Tickets agencies (look under "ticket offices") or go to www.prague-info.cz.

Where it all happens

Everything happens in the relatively small area between the New Town and the Old Town, which means you can enjoy a number of venues in one evening. Make sure you investigate the Malá Strana as well. When you cross Charles Bridge at night, you'll have a fantastic view of the Castle illuminated in all its splendor. Entry to the nightclubs isn't expensive and the drinks are equally reasonable.

What to wear

A night out in Prague is an important event, and people dress up for the occasion. You shouldn't turn up at the Opera or theater in casual clothes. There's no need to wear a long dress or dinner jacket, but it's important to look smart. Take a look around the lobby in the interval for a spot of interesting people watching. If you're headed for a jazz club or nightclub you can be more relaxed about your attire.

FINDING YOUR WAY

You will find details of the nearest metro station or tram after the address in the Going Out section. Many venues now have websites where you can usually find detailed directions and often a map of how to get there.

Jeans, leather, tattoos and body piercing are all widely sported.

Traveling around at night

The metro operates from 5am to midnight, and many night trams run from midnight to 5am. They all pass by Lazarská and Spálená in the New Town and start with the number 5.

Tourists sometimes have trouble with some taxi drivers who overcharge. It is wise to use well-known companies such as AAA whose cars have the logo of the firm written on the door of the vehicle (☎ 14014 – English spoken).

Safety

Prague is a safe city, even at night. Tourists are unlikely to encounter any animosity or aggressive behavior. However, do beware of pickpockets and never be tempted to change money on the black market. Don't wear your most valuable jewelry, and make sure you take care of your bag, backpack, camera and camcorder. Leave your passport at the hotel, unless changing money – you won't need it during the day.

Where to buy tickets

You can buy tickets in advance from the box office at the

venues themselves, in some hotels and from the following ticket agencies:

Ticketpro
☎ 296 329 999
www.ticketpro.cz
Rytířská 12
Every day 9am-8pm.

Pražská Informační Služba
Na příkopě 20
☎ 420 12 444
Mon.-Fri. 9am-6pm,
Sat. 9am-3pm
Na Mustku 2, every day
9am-8pm.

Bohemia Tickets
www.bohemiaticket.cz
Na příkopě 16
☎ 224 215 031
Mon.-Fri. 10am-7pm,
Sat. 10am-3pm
Male náměstí 13
☎ 224 227 832
Mon.-Fri. 9am-5pm,
Sat. 9am-3pm.

During the tourist season and certain festivals, you may find events are sold out. However, you can often get standby tickets on the night at the box office of the venue concerned.

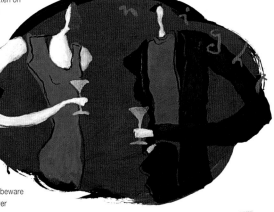

PRAGUE INTERNATIONAL SPRING FESTIVAL

This international festival begins every year on May 12, the anniversary of Smetana's death. It ends three weeks later, on June 2, with Beethoven's *Ninth Symphony*. Prague is in full musical swing during this period, with prestigious concerts and operas taking place, for which you must reserve well in advance. Hundreds of international musicians come to the city to take part. Traditionally, a procession leaves from Smetana's grave in Vyšehrad and heads to the Municipal House, where his most famous work, *Má vlast* (My Fatherland), is performed.

Information:
Hellichova 18
☎ 257 312 547, ☏ 257 313 725
www.festival.cz
Tickets sold by the Ticketpro agency.

Classical music

1 - Stavoské divadlo
2 - Sv. Mikuláš
3 - Sv. Jakuba
4 - Stavoské divadlo

In Prague, music takes pride of place and you'll be spoiled for choice if you wish to attend a concert or an opera, late in the afternoon or in the evening. Theaters, churches and concert halls are pure showcases and seat prices are nowhere near as expensive as those in London or Paris. At the opera, the productions can be as daring as they are traditional, but the performance is always of high quality thanks to the existence of uniformly good companies. There are few international stars, but good casts who show the works and the composers to their advantage. Churches and concert halls present numerous and interesting programs even though they are not always very original. However, beware of shows publicized through flyers handed out on the street. They are intended for tourists and can be of poor quality.

Národní divadlo (National Theater)

Národní třída 2
Metro: Národní třída
☎ 224 912 673
www.narodni-divadlo.cz
Every day 10am-6pm; tickets:
Ostrovní, 1 or Ovocný trh, 6.

This imposing building, to which a modern wing with rather surprising architecture was added in the 1980s, offers a different show every evening: plays (in Czech, of course), concerts, ballets or operas.

Státní opera Praha (State Opera)

Wilsonova 4
Metro: Muzeum
☎ 224 227 266
www.opera.cz
Mon.-Fri. 10am-5.30pm, Sat.-
Sun. 10am-noon and 1-5.30pm;

and an hour before the show; also via Bohemia Tickets.

Opened in 1888, the biggest theater in Prague is as imposing as the one in Vienna, of which it is a smaller copy. Its repertoire is worthy of a great international theater and performances takes place nearly every evening.

Stavoské divadlo (Estate Theater)

Ovocný trh. 1
Metro: Můstek
☎ 224 901 487
www.narodni-divadlo.cz
Every day 10am-6pm;
Tickets at the Kolowrat Palace (Ovocný trh, 6).

It is in this magical theater that the marvelous *Don Giovanni* by Mozart was opened (see p. 55). His great operas are rightfully permanently on the program, especially for the weekend matinée or evening performances. Note that it is difficult to reserve seats here just before the performance.

Concert halls

Obecní dům, Smetana Hall

Náměstí Republiky 5
Metro: Náměstí Republiky
☎ 222 002 101
www.obecnidum.cz
Tickets at venue every day 10am-6pm or from Ticketpro.

The Obecní dům (Municipal House, see p. 55) houses the prestigious Smetana concert hall, one of the largest halls in Prague with 1,500 seats. Decorated with sculptures and frescoes devoted to the Czech composers, it regularly welcomes the Prague symphony orchestra.

Dům U kamenného zvonu

Staroměstské náměstí 13
Metro: Můstek
☎ 224 22 43 51
Every day 7.30pm
Tickets at venue or from Ticketpro (every day 10am-6pm).

Only chamber music is performed in this Gothic 14th-century building, and you'll be served a glass of Czech champagne (*Sekt*).

Rudolfinum

Náměstí Jana Palacha
Metro: Staroměstská
Tickets: Listopadu 17, at the corner of Náměstí Jana Palacha,
☎ 227 059 227
www.rudofinum.cz
Mon.-Fri. 10am-6pm, and one hour before each concert.

The Filharmonie Česká, the most prestigious orchestra in the country, gave its first concert here on January 4, 1896, conducted by Dvořák. Today in residence in this very theater, it performs numerous concerts of high standard. These also offer the opportunity to discover the Dvořák

Hall, as imposing as the main building itself.

Churches

Sv. Martin ve zdi

Martinská
Metro: Národní třída
Tickets at venue or from Ticketpro.

At 5 and 7pm every day there are performances by an entire chamber orchestra or the organ alone accompanied by a trumpet. Baroque music and Czech composers dominate the program. You can only visit this church at concert times. Translated, its name is Church of St Martin-in-the-Walls.

Sv. Mikuláš

Malostranské náměstí
Tram 12 or 22, stop: Malostranské náměstí
Tickets at venue.

If you are passing this sumptuous Baroque church at 5pm, feel free to enter and listen to a concert. The acoustics are excellent. Mozart played the St Mikuláš organ with its 2,500 pipes in 1787 and his *Requiem* was played here three years after his death.

Sv. Jakuba

Malá Štupartská 6
Metro: Náměstí Republiky
Tickets at venue or from Ticketpro.

Equipped with an organ of excellent quality, this superb Baroque church is renowned for its acoustics and its Baroque Christmas Mass, *Česká mše vánoční Hej Mistře*, celebrated on December 24 at midnight and on December 26 at 10.30am. The program is displayed outside the church and the concerts take place at 6pm.

Jazz

1 - U Staré Paní
2 - Agharta Jazz Centrum
3 - U Malého Glena
4 - Reduta Jazz Club

The Americans introduced jazz to Prague after World War I, and it has now become something of a tradition in the city. The New Orleans sound has been heard in the jazz clubs since the '50s. Today's talented musicians, among them Emil Vicklický and Karel Růžička, combine all the styles and have even made a name for themselves abroad. In Prague itself Emil and Karel are part of the fashionable club scene and play alongside international artists. Concerts usually start around 9pm, and the programs are eclectic but mostly of excellent quality. Jazz lovers won't be disappointed.

Agharta Jazz Centrum

Železná 16
Metro: Můstek
☎ 222 211 275
www.agharta.cz
Bar: every day 6pm-1am;
concerts every day 9-11.30pm.

This club was founded in 1911 and, as the organizer of the international Prague Jazz Festival, it is generally considered to be the city's best jazz club and is certainly one of the most popular. Located since 2004 in beautiful vaulted rooms with exposed stonework, a large part of its varied program is devoted to quality Czech ensembles. Among the Czech artists regularly invited, you may be lucky enough to listen to the Emil Viklický Trio or Jiří Stivin & Co. The club also has a shop selling a large selection of CDs, among which are compilations with the title The Best of Agharta, as well as an attractive Agharta T-Shirt by Jiří Votruba.

Prague Jazz Festival

www.agharta.cz/festprog.htm

The annual international jazz festival takes place in October and attracts some big names. Since 1964, the Agharta and Lucerna clubs have welcomed such major artists as BB King, Chick Corea, The Brecker Brothers, Jan Garbarek, Wynton Marsalis, Maceo Parker and Pat Metheny. It is a good idea to reserve a table from Agharta or Ticketpro (see p. 125). Huge crowds are drawn to the clubs when the festival is on.

(see p. 125)

Metropolitan Jazz Club

Jungmannova 14
Metro: Národní třída
☎ 224 947 777
Every day 11am-1am, concerts at 9pm; in summer only open from 7pm.

There are only five tables in this small jazz restaurant, located in a pretty courtyard adjoining Vodičkova. The music tends to be traditional, as does the menu. Enjoy your meal or sip a cocktail as you listen to the music, which starts at 9pm. It is advisable to get there early to secure a table.

U Staré Paní

Michalská 9
Metro: Můstek
☎ 603 551 680
www.jazzinprague.com
Every day 7pm-2am, concerts at 9pm.

In the basement of a restored house (the rest of the building houses a hotel and a restaurant with the same name), this jazz lounge offers an eclectic, excellent-quality program. In a modern and colorful decor, you can listen to the concert at a table or at the bar, while you just have a drink (wide choice of wines) or while you treat yourself to simple, light dishes, salads or sandwiches.

U Malého Glena

Karmelitská 23
Tram 12 or 22, stop: Malostranské náměstí
☎ 257 531 717
www.malyglen.cz
Every day 8pm-2am, concerts Mon.-Fri. 9.30pm-1am, Sat.-Sun. 10pm-1am.

Start your evening with a Tex-Mex meal in this atmospheric pub on the first floor. After your

meal, go downstairs into the basement, where the rather eclectic program alternates between jazz on Saturdays and Sundays, acid jazz on Thursdays and blues or Latin American music on other days. Arrive early or reserve a table as it is a small, popular venue.

Reduta Jazz Club

Národní 20
Metro: Národní třída
☎ 224 933 487
www.redutajazzclub.cz
Every day 9pm-midnight.

Undoubtedly the most famous club in Prague since the 1960s (it has just celebrated its 45th anniversary) the Reduta is located in the basement of a charming art-nouveau house. Very popular with tourists, it remains a prestigious place where the great Czech stars, such as Emil Viklický, Jana Koublova and Milan Svoboda, give performances. Its excellent program is quite varied and sometimes exceptional: In 1994, Bill Clinton and Václav Havel performed an improvised jam session, the former playing the sax and the latter the drums (the CD of this unforgettable jam session is still on sale here).

Jazz Café c. 14

Opatovická 14
Metro: Národní třída
☎ 224 934 674
Mon.-Fri. noon-11pm, Sat.-Sun. 5pm-11pm.

There is a friendly, warm atmosphere in this jazz café with its posters of great jazz artists on the walls. It is rather unusually furnished with gaming tables from the 1950s alongside some antique sewing machines. The venue also has somewhat subdued lighting, but nevertheless a certain charm. It is a great place for a rendezvous with a few friends to get in the right mood before a concert. You can enjoy a salad or indulge in a few canapés before the night really begins. The Jazz Café is a perfect venue to start your big night out in Prague.

Black light theater,
mime and puppets

1 - Ta Fantastika
2 - Divadlo Image

Černé divadlo Jiřího Srnce

Národní 20
☎ 602 291 572
www.blacktheatresrnec.cz
Every day 7.30pm, tickets at
venue Mon.-Fri. 3-7.30pm,
Sat.-Sun. from 7pm.

Created in 1961 by Jiří Srnec, this was the first black light theater in the world. The actors are dressed all in black against a black backdrop, making them invisible when manipulating puppets or objects and thus able to perform their visual trickery. The talented company performs extracts from shows devised by the inventive Srnec

The first Pierrot was the creation of Jean-Baptiste Gaspard Deburau, the son of a Czech mother and a French father, born in 1796 in Kolín in Bohemia. Ever since, the art of the mime has been an important part of Czech cultural heritage. Today, the

Ladislav Fialka troupe continues this tradition. Fialka, who was born in 1931 and died in 1991, was a real master of mime. His troupe tours the world with his imaginative creations. The Czech school of mime is constantly developing and embracing new techniques.

who is worshipped by most Czechs. A great pick-me-up!

Černé divadlo Františka Kratochvíla – Divadlo Reduta

Národní 25
☎ 221 085 276

www.divadlometro.cz
Tickets at venue Mon.-Sat. 4-8pm.

The program here alternates between *Miss Sony*, a comical farce about love, and the famous *Anatomy of a Kiss*, a humorous and poetic depiction of the relationship between a man and a woman, in which a simple drawing becomes real.

All Colors Theater

Rytířská 31
☎ 221 610 173
www.blacktheatre.cz
Tickets at venue every day 10am-7pm; reservations: ☎ 221 610 173; performances at 8.30pm.

The All Colors Theater performs three shows with black light

theater, movies, dance and musical comedy in an intentionally kitsch production. *The Magic Universe* is a journey into the depths of time, while *Faust* tells the story of the man who made a pact with the devil. *Concert in Black Light* introduces variations on the works of Haydn, Mozart and Vranický.

Černé divadlo a pantomina – Divadlo Image

Pařížská 4
☎ 222 314 448
Tickets at venue every day 9am-8pm or www.imagetheatre.cz; performances at 8pm.

This black light theater venue, staging mime and modern dance, attracts crowds of tourists thanks to its location a stone's throw from the Old Town Square.

Ta Fantastika – Palac Unitaria

Karlova 8
☎ 222 221 366
www.tafantastika.cz
Tickets at venue every day 11am-9.30pm.

Enjoy a mixture of cartoons, puppet movies, and action and erotic movies at this exciting black light theater venue. *Gulliver* is an adaptation of the works of Jonathan Swift and Jack London. *Alice* could easily be entitled *Alice in the Land of Special Effects*.

Puppet Theaters

Puppet theater has a very long tradition at the heart of the country's culture (see p. 20) and it would be a shame not to see a puppet show during your stay in Prague.

Špejbl and Hurvínek

Dejvická 38
☎ 233 341 241
Reservations: ☎ 224 316 784
Box office: Tue.-Fri. 10am-2pm, 3-6pm.

This is the most famous puppet show in the city. The story revolves around a narrow-minded father, Špejbl, and Hurvínek, his reprobate son, who is an intellectual extrovert. These characters have been made famous by television cartoons and are responsible for breaking down the traditional barriers of children's puppet theater. Enjoy the comic performance, and then go and treat yourself to one

of the puppets so that you'll never forget the event (see Shopping pp. 100-101).

Laterna Magika

Národní třída 4
☎ 224 931 482
Tickets at venue Mon.-Sat. 10am-8pm, ☎ 224 914 129; performances 8pm.

Magic Lantern founded multimedia theater back in 1958, and their success has been huge ever since. They create a wonderful world of illusion and special effects.

Nightclubs
and live venues

1 - Marquis de Sade (p. 134)
2 - Jo's Bar & Jo's Garaz
3 - Molly Malones Irish Pub
   (p. 134)
4 - La Casa Blu

Kavárna v sedmém nebi

Zborovská 68
Tram 6, 9, 22 and 23, stop: Újezd
☎ 257 318 110
Every day 10am-1am.

This is a small mezzanine bar near the Vltava popular with young Czechs. Pleasant setting. Good music. The bar offers sandwiches and toast in a relaxed atmosphere. A good place to relax in the early evening as well as for late-night drinking.

Malá Strana

Jo's Bar & Jo's Garaz

Malostranské náměstí 7
Tram 12 or 22, stop:
Malostranské nám.
☎ 257 531 422
Every day 11am-2am.

If you feel like a coffee or something to drink, or if you want to dance until the small hours, seek out this inviting establishment under the arcades facing St Nicholas's church. On the first floor, a busy narrow American bar leads at the back into a small and quieter room where you can also have sandwiches, salads and Tex-Mex dishes. In the basement you can dance to pop music (until 5am) in a beautiful vaulted room. The atmosphere is relaxed, even though tourists outnumber Czechs.

Malostranská Beseda

Malostranské náměstí 21
Tram 12 or 22, stop:
Malostranské nám.
☎ 257 53 20 92
Every day 11am-10pm.

Take the stairs to the second floor, where you'll find several local rock groups performing Czech-style 1960s and 1970s music in the small concert room. This venue has a real Czech flavor and an unusually minimalist decor. However, there are often some interesting local paintings and photographs on the walls which liven up the scene. Arrive early when the atmosphere is very lively.

Klub Újezd

Újzed 18
Tram 12 or 22, stop: Újezd
☎ 257 316 537
Every day 2pm-4am.

The first private club to open after the Velvet Revolution, today it is the favorite haunt of Prague's "grunge" youth. On the first floor there is a tiny space that doubles as a nightclub and concert venue. On the second floor there is a smoky bar with very noisy music. The young people here are not generally too active. They'll be munching on canapés and shouldn't be disturbed.

Hergetova Cihelna (The Brickyard)

Cihelna 2b, Prague 1
☎ 257 535 534
Every day 10am-midnight.

This is the latest fashionable address and the most recent creation of the KampaGroup which manages several restaurants in Malá Strana. The restored brickyard dates back to the Middle Ages and opens onto the river. It has become a very fashionable place with restaurants, bars and museums. There is a superb view of Charles Bridge. The decor is evironmentally friendly, using wood and bamboo. The music is soft and the atmosphere refined. Early brunches are also served for parents who like to relax, with a nursery for the children. Unique in Prague.

Futurum

Zborovská 7
☎ 257 32 85 71
Every day 8pm-3am.

This rather dreary former nightclub has had a complete makeover and it now attracts a young Czech clientele that goes wild on Fridays at the 1980s and 1990s nights: The young people dance under a giant TV screen showing old video clips. The bar also hosts a variety of live bands.

Staré Město

Café Indigo

Platnerska 11
Metro: Staroměstská
Mon.-Fri. 9am-midnight,
Sat.-Sun. noon-midnight.

With its bare and faded walls brightened up here and there with contemporary paintings, its visible pipes and ducts and its metal bar, this big pub with its industrial design is highly rated by the students of the neighboring university. Though the very bright main room opening onto the street is the very image of a cafeteria of the 1980s, the room at the back is more cozy. People come here in the daytime to have a coffee or a tea, or in the evenings to have a glass of wine or a beer. You can also eat here (salads, soups, snacks, etc.) at very affordable prices.

Four Seasons Piano Bar

Veleslavínova 2a
☎ 221 427 000.

After mingling with the crowds during the day on Charles Bridge, relax on a comfortable sofa in the bar of the Four Seasons. Cozy atmosphere, soft piano jazz and faultless service. Music from 6pm to midnight.

Blatouch-Café Bar

Vězeňská 4
Metro: Staroměstská
☎ 222 328 643
Mon.-Thu. 11am-midnight, Fri. 11am-2am, Sat.-Sun. 2pm-1am.

The Edward Hopper paintings on the walls add to the literary atmosphere of this bar, with its

shelves full of books. You can enjoy an intimate conversation in the friendly atmosphere while sipping a cocktail (alcoholic or nonalcoholic) and enjoying a salad or sandwich.

La Casa Blu

Kozí 15
Metro: Staroměstská
☎ 224 818 270
Mon.-Sat. 11am-midnight,
Sun. 2pm-midnight.

La Casa Blu is wonderful on a cold winter's night in the city. With sombreros on the ocher walls and tequila or rum cocktails, this is a great place to come to listen to Latin American music. You can chat with the owner Pepi and you're always sure to get a friendly reception.

Marquis de Sade

Templova 8
Metro: Můstek or Náměstí Republiky
☎ 224 817 505
Every day 11am-3am.

This large bar, with its high ceilings, red walls and long tables, has little to do with the Marquis himself, but it draws a mostly expatriate crowd. It's a good place to start the evening, and the atmosphere is always lively. However, sometimes the quality of the food can be a little unreliable.

Molly Malones Irish Pub

U Obecního dvora 4
Metro: Staroměstská
☎ 224 818 851
Sun.-Thu. 11am-1am,
Fri.-Sat. 11am-2am.

Another Irish pub, with an open fire, draft Guinness and cider, hot food, Irish music, Irish staff, rickety tables and an eclectic decor. The dedicated beer and whiskey drinkers stand at the bar, and there are small concerts from time to time. You'll feel as if you've discovered a piece of Ireland right in the heart of Bohemia.

Kolkovna

V Kolkovné 8, Josefov
Metro: Staroměstská
☎ 224 819 701
Every day 11am-midnight.

In this pub, beer takes pride of place in the mugs as well as on the walls. The design of the pub is both traditional and refined:

green walls enhanced by wood paneling, a superb copper and wood bar, wooden tables and high stools. The waiters dressed in black and white with green aprons carry out their service perfectly for a rather upscale clientele. You can eat tasty snacks in the bar, but note that there is also a chic restaurant in the basement.

Roxy

Dlouhá 33
Metro: Náměstí Republiky
☎ 224 826 296
Every day 11am-1am.

Formerly a theater, traces of which can still be seen on the

dance floor. It is also thought to have been the site of the first public film show. Nowadays, Roxy is the scene of much musical and theatrical experimentation, and it's a must on the list of things to do at night in Prague. Enjoy a really delicious vegetarian couscous while listening to techno music.

Nové Město

Défilé

Vodičkova 17
Metro: Můstek
☎ 296 249 020
Mon.-Fri. from 8am, Sat.-Sun. from 10am.

This fashionable bar and lounge on two levels is an "in" place. White or natural brick

walls, leather sofas, designer furniture and TV screens showing fashion parades create an original and relaxed atmosphere. The great choice of drinks and snacks is listed in a very original menu. In the basement, from 10pm onward every night, a DJ insures you'll have fun. Disco nights Thursday through Saturday.

Lucerna bar

Lucerna, Vodičkova 36
Metro: Můstek or Muzeum
☎ 224 21 71 08
Every day 8pm-3am.

On Saturday nights there are 1960s or 1980s evenings at this bar, and the lively clientele can be very exuberant. It is the biggest club in the city, and has a varied program, so it is certainly worth a visit. You might even catch some great live jazz performances.

Radost FX

Bělehradská 120
Metro: I.P. Pavlova
☎ 224 25 47 76
Every day 11am-5am.

The vegetarian restaurant on the first floor serves food until 4am. Choose from generous dishes of pasta, lasagne and salads with a sweet vinaigrette dressing. A musician sometimes makes an appearance in one of the two lounge-style rooms

1 - Kolkovna
2 - Défilé
3 - Radost FX
4 - Akropolis

behind the restaurant, one of which is nonsmoking. The basement decor is psychedelic and techno music is played here until 5am by tireless DJs. Those looking for a more sedate time can enjoy comfortable chairs and snacks upstairs.

U Sudu

Vodičkova 10
Metro: Karlovo náměstí
Mon.-Fri. 11am-midnight,
Sat.-Sun. 2pm-midnight.

There is a heady mix of wine and beer fumes in this bar, which has several basement rooms. It's an authentic *vinárna* and a favorite with young Czechs, who enjoy the dark rooms and loud rock music. In summer, a few tables are set up outside. If you're here in early fall try a glass of *burčák* (young wine) with a *chlebíčky* (fresh open sandwich), available any time.

Duplex

Václavské náměstí 21
Metro: Můstek
☎ 224 232 319
Café-bar: every day 10am-midnight
Club: Wed.-Sat. 10pm-5am.

Two elevators take you directly up to the 7th floor, in a post-modern setting where wood, bricks and girders are enhanced with white flowing curtains and cushions, red upholstery and white and red Panton chairs. It is terribly kitsch, but the terrace offers unrestricted views over the city. A good place to come and have a drink before going to the club for a theme party.

Žižkov

Akropolis

Kubelíkova 27
Metro: Jiřího z Poděbrad
☎ 296 330 911
www.palicakropolis.cz
Mon.-Sat. 4pm-2am,
Sun. 4pm-midnight.

This first-floor bar is on the corner of the street and it is always busy in the evening. Enjoy a selection of local and vegetarian dishes and admire the rather surreal aquarium, fully equipped with sand and a giant compass. Just to the right as you leave you'll find a former movie house in the basement that has been converted into a theater. The program is both varied and original, and includes plays and musical concerts.

Metric Conversion Chart

Women's sizes

Shirts/dresses

U.K.	U.S.A.	EUROPE
8	6	36
10	8	38
12	10	40
14	12	42
16	14	44
18	16	46

Sweaters

U.K.	U.S.A.	EUROPE
8	6	44
10	8	46
12	10	48
14	12	50
16	14	52

Shoes

U.K.	U.S.A.	EUROPE
3	5	36
4	6	37
5	7	38
6	8	39
7	9	40
8	10	41

Men's sizes

Shirts

U.K.	U.S.A.	EUROPE
14	14	36
$14^{1/2}$	$14^{1/2}$	37
15	15	38
$15^{1/2}$	$15^{1/2}$	39
16	16	41
$16^{1/2}$	$16^{1/2}$	42
17	17	43
$17^{1/2}$	$17^{1/2}$	44
18	18	46

Suits

U.K.	U.S.A.	EUROPE
36	36	46
38	38	48
40	40	50
42	42	52
44	44	54
46	46	56

Shoes

U.K.	U.S.A.	EUROPE
6	8	39
7	9	40
8	10	41
9	10.5	42
10	11	43
11	12	44
12	13	45

More useful conversions

1 centimeter	0.39 inches	1 inch	2.54 centimeters
1 meter	1.09 yards	1 yard	0.91 meters
1 kilometer	0.62 miles	1 mile	1. 61 kilometers
1 liter	2.12 (US) pints	1 (US) pint	0.47 liters
1 gram	0.035 ounces	1 ounce	28.35 grams
1 kilogram	2.2 pounds	1 pound	0.45 kilograms

Published by AA Travel Publishing.

First published as Un grand week-end à Prague: © Hachette Livre (Hachette Tourisme), 2005
Written by Florence Lejeune, Carole Vantroys and Jean-Yves Cotté
Maps within the book © Hachette Tourisme

Published by AA Publishing, a trading name of Automobile Association Developments Limited, whose registered office is Fanum House, Basing View, Basingstoke, Hampshire RG21 4EA. Registered number 1878835.

ISBN-10: 0-7495-4841-X
ISBN-13: 978-0-7495-4841-4

The contents of this publication are believed correct at the time of printing. Nevertheless, AA Publishing accept no responsibility for errors, omissions or changes in the details given, or for the consequences of readers' reliance on this information. This does not affect your statutory rights. Assessments of the attractions, hotels and restaurants are based upon the author's own experience and contain subjective opinions that may reflect the publisher's opinion or a reader's experience. We have tried to ensure accuracy, but things do change, so please let us know if you have any comments or corrections.

Original English translation by Jane Moseley and Anthony Moinet © Hachette Livre (Hachette Tourisme), 2005
Additional translation work by G and W Advertising and Publishing © Automobile Association Developments Limited 2006

Cover design by Bookwork Creative Associates, Hampshire
Cover maps produced from map data © MAIRDUMONT/Falk Verlag 2005

Colour separation by Kingsclere Design and Print
Printed and bound in China by Leo Paper Products

Cover credits

Front cover: AA World Travel Library/Clive Sawyer; **Back cover**: Laurent Parrault

Picture Credits

Laurent Parrault: pp. 4, 11 (c.), 12 (t l., b.), 14 (b.), 18 (b.), 20 (b.), 22 (t r., b.), 23 (t), 24 (t l., b.),, 25 (t), 28 (t r.), 29 (c.), 30, 34, 35, 37 (t, c.), 38 (t), 40, 41 (c.), 42 (b.), 45 (c. c.), 46, 47 (t l.), 48 (t. r.), 50, 51 (b.), 53 (t), 54 (b.), 55 (t), 57 (c.), 59 (c.), 61 (b.), 62 (t, c.), 64, 65 (t l., c.), 67 (b. l.), 68, 69, 70, 71, 72, 73, 74, 75, 76, 77, 78, 79, 80, 82 (t l., t r.), 83 (t), 85 (t r., c. r.), 86 (t l., t r., c. c.), 87, 89, 90, 91, 92, 94, 95, 96, 97, 98, 99, 100, 101, 104 (t l., b.), 105, 106 (t r., b.), 107, 108 (t r., b.), 109 (t), 110 (b.), 112 (t l., c., b.), 113, 114 (t r.), 115 (t l.), 118, 119 (t, c. c., b.), 120 (t r., b.), 121 (b.), 122 (b.), 123, 124, 126 (c. l.), 128 (t r.), 129 (b.), 131 (c. r.), 132 (t l., c. c., c. r.), 135.
Éric Guillot: pp.2 (b.), 3 (b.), 10 (t l.), 13 (c.), 14 (t l.), 15 (c. r.), 18 (t), 19, 20 (t r.), 21 (b.), 22 (t l.), 23 (b.), 24 (t r.), 26 (t r.), 28 (t l.), 29 (t), 38 (c.), 39 (c.), 43, 44 (b. r.), 45 (t, c. r.), 47 (t r.), 48 (b.), 49 (t, c. l.), 51 (b.), 53 (c., b.), 54 (t), 55 (c.), 59 (t, b.), 60, 53 (t, c.), 66, 67 (t r.), 82 (c. c., c. r.), 83 (b.), 84, 85 (t l., c. c.), 86 (c. r.), 88, 102, 103, 104 (t r.), 106 (t l.), 108 (t r.), 109 (c. r., c. c.), 110 (t), 111, 112 (t r.), 114 (t l., b.), 115 (t r.), 116, 117, 119 (c. r.), 120 (t l.), 121 (c.), 122 (t), 126 (t l., c. r.), 127, 128 (c. l., c. r.), 130, 131 (t, b.), 132 (t r.), 133.
Pawel Wysocki, Hémisphères: pp. 3 (t), 10 (t r., b.), 12 (t r.), 13 (t), 14 (t r.), 15 (b.), 16 (t r., b.), 17, 20 (t l.), 21 (t), 27 (t), 37 (b.), 38 (b.), 41 (t, b.), 44 (b. l.), 51 (t), 56, 57 (t), 58, 61 (c.), 62 (b.), 63 (b.), 65 (t r.), 126 (t r.), 134.
Gil Giulio, Hémisphères: pp. 28 (b.), 42 (t r.), 47 (b.), 49 (c. r.), 61 (t).
Philippe Renault: pp. 3 (c.), 25 (b.), 27 (c.), 36, 39 (t), 52, 55 (b.), 67 (b. r.).
Hachette Livre: pp. 11 (t l.), 15 (t c.), 16 (t l.), 26 (t l., b.).

Illustrations

Monique Prudent

A02680